JavaScript Patterns

Stoyan Stefanov

O'REILLY®

Beijing · Cambridge · Farnham · Köln · Sebastopol · Tokyo

JavaScript Patterns
by Stoyan Stefanov

Published by O'Reilly Media, Inc., 1005 Gravenstein Highway North, Sebastopol, CA 95472.

O'Reilly books may be purchased for educational, business, or sales promotional use. Online editions are also available for most titles (*http://my.safaribooksonline.com*). For more information, contact our corporate/institutional sales department: (800) 998-9938 or *corporate@oreilly.com*.

Editor: Mary Treseler	**Indexer:** Potomac Indexing, LLC
Production Editor: Teresa Elsey	**Cover Designer:** Karen Montgomery
Copyeditor: ContentWorks, Inc.	**Interior Designer:** David Futato
Proofreader: Teresa Elsey	**Illustrator:** Robert Romano

September 2010:   First Edition.

Revision History for the First Edition:
2010-09-08	First release
2010-11-12	Second release
2011-10-21	Third release
2012-11-02	Fourth release

See *http://oreilly.com/catalog/errata.csp?isbn=9780596806750* for release details.

ISBN: 978-0-596-80675-0

[LSI]

1351870562

To my girls: Eva, Zlatina, and Nathalie

Table of Contents

Preface

Patterns are solutions to common problems. One step further, patterns are templates for solving categories of problems.

Patterns help you split a problem into Lego-like blocks and focus on the unique parts of the problem while abstracting out a lot of "been there, done that, got the T-shirt" kind of details.

Patterns also help us communicate better by simply providing a common vocabulary.

It's therefore important to identify and study patterns.

Target Audience

This book is not a beginner's book; it's targeted at professional developers and programmers who want to take their JavaScript skills to the next level.

Some of the basics (like loops, conditionals, and closures) are not discussed at all. If you find you need to brush up on some of those topics, refer to the list of suggested reading.

At the same time, some topics (such as object creation or hoisting) may look too basic to be in this book, but they are discussed from a patterns perspective and, in my opinion, are critical to harnessing the power of the language.

If you're looking for best practices and powerful patterns to help you write better, maintainable, robust JavaScript code, this book is for you.

Conventions Used in This Book

The following typographical conventions are used in this book:

Italic
: Indicates new terms, URLs, email addresses, filenames, and file extensions.

Constant width

> Used for program listings, as well as within paragraphs to refer to program elements such as variable or function names, databases, data types, environment variables, statements, and keywords.

Constant width bold

> Shows commands or other text that should be typed literally by the user.

Constant width italic

> Shows text that should be replaced with user-supplied values or by values determined by context.

 This icon signifies a tip, suggestion, or general note.

 This icon signifies a warning or caution.

Using Code Examples

This book is here to help you get your job done. In general, you may use the code in this book in your programs and documentation. You do not need to contact us for permission unless you're reproducing a significant portion of the code. For example, writing a program that uses several chunks of code from this book does not require permission. Selling or distributing a CD-ROM of examples from O'Reilly books does require permission. Answering a question by citing this book and quoting example code does not require permission. Incorporating a significant amount of example code from this book into your product's documentation does require permission.

We appreciate, but do not require, attribution. An attribution usually includes the title, author, publisher, and ISBN. For example: "*JavaScript Patterns*, by Stoyan Stefanov (O'Reilly). Copyright 2010 Yahoo!, Inc., 9780596806750."

If you feel your use of code examples falls outside fair use or the permission given here, feel free to contact us at *permissions@oreilly.com*.

Safari® Books Online

 Safari Books Online is an on-demand digital library that lets you easily search over 7,500 technology and creative reference books and videos to find the answers you need quickly.

With a subscription, you can read any page and watch any video from our library online. Read books on your cell phone and mobile devices. Access new titles before they are available for print, and get exclusive access to manuscripts in development and post feedback for the authors. Copy and paste code samples, organize your favorites, download chapters, bookmark key sections, create notes, print out pages, and benefit from tons of other time-saving features.

O'Reilly Media has uploaded this book to the Safari Books Online service. To have full digital access to this book and others on similar topics from O'Reilly and other publishers, sign up for free at *http://my.safaribooksonline.com*.

How to Contact Us

Please address comments and questions concerning this book to the publisher:

> O'Reilly Media, Inc.
> 1005 Gravenstein Highway North
> Sebastopol, CA 95472
> 800-998-9938 (in the United States or Canada)
> 707-829-0515 (international or local)
> 707-829-0104 (fax)

We have a web page for this book, where we list errata, examples, and any additional information. You can access this page at:

> *http://oreilly.com/catalog/9780596806750*

To comment or ask technical questions about this book, send email to:

> *bookquestions@oreilly.com*

For more information about our books, conferences, Resource Centers, and the O'Reilly Network, see our website at:

> *http://oreilly.com*

Acknowledgments

I am forever indebted to the incredible reviewers who shared their energy and knowledge to make a much better book for the good of the community. Their blogs and Twitter streams are a constant source of awe, sharp observations, great ideas, and patterns.

- Dmitry Soshnikov (*http://dmitrysoshnikov.com*, @DmitrySoshnikov)
- Andrea Giammarchi (*http://webreflection.blogspot.com*, @WebReflection)
- Asen Bozhilov (*http://asenbozhilov.com*, @abozhilov)
- Juriy Zaytsev (*http://perfectionkills.com*, @kangax)

- Ryan Grove (*http://wonko.com*, @yaypie)
- Nicholas Zakas (*http://nczonline.net*, @slicknet)
- Remy Sharp (*http://remysharp.com*, @rem)
- Iliyan Peychev

Credits

Some of the patterns in the book were identified by the author, based on experience and on studies of popular JavaScript libraries such as jQuery and YUI. But most of the patterns are identified and described by the JavaScript community; therefore, this book is a result of the collective work of many developers. To not interrupt the narrative with history and credits, a list of references and suggested additional reading is given on the book's companion site at *http://www.jspatterns.com/book/reading/*.

If I've missed a good and original article in the list of references, please accept my apologies and contact me so I can add it to the online list at *http://jspatterns.com*.

Reading

This is not a beginner's book and some basic topics such as loops and conditions are skipped. If you need to learn more about the language, following are some suggested titles:

- *Object-Oriented JavaScript* by yours truly (Packt Publishing)
- *JavaScript: The Definitive Guide* by David Flanagan (O'Reilly)
- *JavaScript: The Good Parts* by Douglas Crockford (O'Reilly)
- *Pro JavaScript Design Patterns* by Ross Hermes and Dustin Diaz (Apress)
- *High Performance JavaScript* by Nicholas Zakas (O'Reilly)
- *Professional JavaScript for Web Developers* by Nicholas Zakas (Wrox)

CHAPTER 1

Introduction

JavaScript is the language of the Web. It started as a way to manipulate a few selected types of elements in a web page (such as images and form fields), but it has grown tremendously. In addition to client-side browser scripting, these days you can use JavaScript to program for an increasing variety of platforms. You can write server-side code (using .NET or Node.js), desktop applications (that work on all operating systems) and application extensions (e.g., for Firefox or Photoshop), mobile applications, and command-line scripts.

JavaScript is also an unusual language. It doesn't have classes, and functions are first-class objects used for many tasks. Initially the language was considered deficient by many developers, but in more recent years these sentiments have changed. Interestingly, languages such as Java and PHP started adding features such as closures and anonymous functions, which JavaScript developers have been enjoying and taking for granted for a while.

JavaScript is dynamic enough that you can make it look and feel like another language you're already comfortable with. But the better approach is to embrace its differences and study its specific patterns.

Patterns

A pattern in the broader sense of the word is a "theme of recurring events or objects... it can be a template or model which can be used to generate things" (*http://en.wikipedia .org/wiki/Pattern*).

In software development, a pattern is a solution to a common problem. A pattern is not necessarily a code solution ready for copy-and-paste but more of a best practice, a useful abstraction, and a template for solving categories of problems.

It is important to identify patterns because:

- They help us write better code using proven practices and not reinvent the wheel.
- They provide a level of abstraction—the brain can hold only so much at a given time, so when you think about a more complex problem, it helps if you don't bother with the low-level details but account for them with self-contained building blocks (patterns).
- They improve communication between developers and teams, which are often in remote locations and don't communicate face to face. Simply putting a label on some coding technique or approach makes it easier to make sure we're talking about the same thing. For example, it's easier to say (and think) "immediate function," than "this thing where you wrap the function in parentheses and at the end of it put another set of parentheses to invoke the function right where you've defined it."

This book discusses the following types of patterns:

- Design patterns
- Coding patterns
- Antipatterns

Design patterns are those initially defined by the "Gang of Four" book (named so after its four authors), originally published in distant 1994 under the title *Design Patterns: Elements of Reusable Object-Oriented Software*. Examples of design patterns are singleton, factory, decorator, observer, and so on. The thing about design patterns in relation to JavaScript is that, although language-independent, the design patterns were mostly studied from the perspective of strongly typed languages, such as C++ and Java. Sometimes it doesn't necessarily make sense to apply them verbatim in a loosely typed dynamic language such as JavaScript. Sometimes these patterns are workarounds that deal with the strongly typed nature of the languages and the class-based inheritance. In JavaScript there might be simpler alternatives. This book discusses JavaScript implementations of several design patterns in Chapter 7.

The *coding patterns* are much more interesting; they are JavaScript-specific patterns and good practices related to the unique features of the language, such as the various uses of functions. JavaScript coding patterns are the main topic of the book.

You might come across an occasional *antipattern* in the book. Antipatterns have a bit of negative or even insulting sound to their name, but that needn't be the case. An antipattern is not the same as a bug or a coding error; it's just a common approach that causes more problems than it solves. Antipatterns are clearly marked with a comment in the code.

JavaScript: Concepts

Let's quickly go over a few important concepts that provide a context for the following chapters.

Object-Oriented

JavaScript is an object-oriented language, which often surprises developers who have previously looked at the language and dismissed it. Anything you look at in a piece of JavaScript code has a good chance of being an object. Only five primitive types are not objects: number, string, boolean, `null`, and `undefined`, and the first three have corresponding object representation in the form of primitive wrappers (discussed in the next chapter). Number, string, and boolean primitive values are easily converted to objects either by the programmer or sometimes behind the scenes by the JavaScript interpreter.

Functions are objects, too. They can have properties and methods.

The simplest thing you do in any language is define a variable. Well, in JavaScript when you define a variable, you're already dealing with objects. First, the variable automatically becomes a *property* of an internal object known as an Activation Object (or a property of the global object if it's a global variable). Second, this variable is actually also object-like because it has its own properties (called *attributes*), which determine whether the variable can be changed, deleted, or enumerated in a `for-in` loop. These attributes are not directly exposed in ECMAScript 3, but edition 5 offers special descriptor methods for manipulating them.

So what are the objects? Because they do so many things they must be quite special. Actually they are extremely simple. An *object* is just a collection of named properties, a list of key-value pairs (almost identical to an associative array in other languages). Some of the properties could be functions (function objects), in which case we call them *methods*.

Another thing about the objects you create is that you can modify them at any time. (Although ECMAScript 5 introduces APIs to prevent mutations.) You can take an object and add, remove, and update its members. If you're concerned about privacy and access, we'll see patterns for this as well.

And one last thing to keep in mind is that there are two main types of objects:

Native
    Described in the ECMAScript standard

Host
    Defined by the host environment (for example, the browser environment)

The *native objects* can further be categorized as *built-in* (for example, `Array`, `Date`) or *user-defined* (`var o = {};`).

Host objects are, for example, `window` and all the DOM objects. If you're wondering whether you're using host objects, try running your code in a different, nonbrowser environment. If it works fine, you're probably using only native objects.

No Classes

You'll see this statement repeated on several occasions throughout the book: There are no classes in JavaScript. This is a novel concept to seasoned programmers in other languages and it takes more than a few repetitions and more than a little effort to "unlearn" classes and accept that JavaScript deals only with objects.

Not having classes makes your programs shorter—you don't need to have a class to create an object. Consider this Java-like object creation:

```
// Java object creation
HelloOO hello_oo = new HelloOO();
```

Repeating the same thing three times looks like an overhead when it comes to creating simple objects. And more often than not, we want to keep our objects simple.

In JavaScript you create a blank object when you need one and then start adding interesting members to it. You compose objects by adding primitives, functions, or other objects to them as their properties. A "blank" object is not entirely blank; it comes with a few built-in properties already but has no "own" properties. We talk about this more in the next chapter.

One of the general rules in the Gang of Four book says, "Prefer object composition to class inheritance." This means that if you can create objects out of available pieces you have lying around, this is a much better approach than creating long parent-child inheritance chains and classifications. In JavaScript it's easy to follow this advice—simply because there are no classes and object composition is what you do anyway.

Prototypes

JavaScript does have inheritance, although this is just one way to reuse code. (And there's an entire chapter on code reuse.) Inheritance can be accomplished in various ways, which usually make use of prototypes. A *prototype* is an object (no surprises) and every function you create automatically gets a `prototype` property that points to a new blank object. This object is almost identical to an object created with an object literal or `Object()` constructor, except that its `constructor` property points to the function you create and not to the built-in `Object()`. You can add members to this blank object and later have other objects inherit from this object and use its properties as their own.

We'll discuss inheritance in detail, but for now just keep in mind that the prototype is an object (not a class or anything special) and every function has a `prototype` property.

Environment

JavaScript programs need an environment to run. The natural habitat for a JavaScript program is the browser, but that's not the only environment. The patterns in the book are mostly related to the core JavaScript (ECMAScript) so they are environment-agnostic. Exceptions are:

- Chapter 8, which specifically deals with browser patterns
- Some other examples that illustrate practical applications of a pattern

Environments can provide their own *host objects*, which are not defined in the ECMA-Script standard and may have unspecified and unexpected behavior.

ECMAScript 5

The core JavaScript programming language (excluding DOM, BOM, and extra host objects) is based on the *ECMAScript* standard, or ES for short. Version 3 of the standard was accepted officially in 1999 and is the one currently implemented across browsers. Version 4 was abandoned and version 5 was approved December 2009, 10 years after the previous.

Version 5 adds some new built-in objects, methods, and properties to the language, but its most important addition is the so-called *strict mode*, which actually removes features from the language, making the programs simpler and less error-prone. For example the usage of the with statement has been disputed over the years. Now in ES5 strict mode it raises an error, although it's okay if found in nonstrict mode. The strict mode is triggered by an ordinary string, which older implementations of the language simply ignore. This means that the usage of strict mode is backward compatible, because it won't raise errors in older browsers that don't understand it.

Once per scope (either function scope, global scope, or at the beginning of a string passed to eval()), you can use the following string:

```
function my() {
    "use strict";
    // rest of the function...
}
```

This means the code in the function is executed in the strict subset of the language. For older browsers this is just a string not assigned to any variable, so it's not used, and yet it's not an error.

The plan for the language is that in the future strict mode will be the only one allowed. In this sense ES5 is a transitional version—developers are encouraged, but not forced, to write code that works in strict mode.

The book doesn't explore patterns related to ES5's specific additions, because at the time of this writing there's no browser that implements ES5. But the examples in this book promote a transition to the new standard by:

- Ensuring the offered code samples will not raise errors in strict mode
- Avoiding and pointing out deprecated constructs such as `arguments.callee`
- Calling out ES3 patterns that have ES5 built-in equivalents such as `Object.create()`

JSLint

JavaScript is an interpreted language with no static compile-time checks. So it's possible to deploy a broken program with a simple typing mistake without realizing it. This is where JSLint helps.

JSLint (*http://jslint.com*) is a JavaScript code quality tool created by Douglas Crockford that inspects your code and warns about potential problems. It's highly recommended that you run your code through JSLint. The tool "will hurt your feelings" as its creator warns, but only in the beginning. You can quickly learn from your mistakes and adopt the essential habits of a professional JavaScript programmer. Having no JSLint error in your code also helps you be more *confident* in the code, knowing that you didn't make a simple omission or syntax error in a hurry.

Starting with the next chapter, you'll see JSLint mentioned a lot. All the code in the book successfully passes JSLint's check (with the default settings, current at the time of writing) except for a few occasions clearly marked as antipatterns.

In its default settings, JSLint expects your code to be strict mode–compliant.

The Console

The `console` object is used throughout the book. This object is not part of the language but part of the environment and is present in most current browsers. In Firefox, for example, it comes with the Firebug extension. The Firebug console has a UI that enables you to quickly type and test little pieces of JavaScript code and also play with the currently loaded page (see Figure 1-1). It's also highly recommended as a learning and exploratory tool. Similar functionality is available in WebKit browsers (Safari and Chrome) as part of the Web Inspector and in IE starting with version 8 as part of Developer Tools.

Most code examples in the book use the `console` object instead of prompting `alert()`s or updating the current page, because it's an easy and unobtrusive way to print some output.

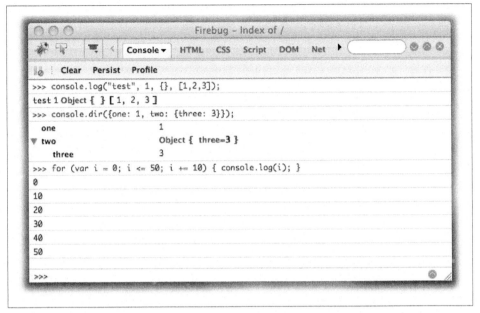

Figure 1-1. Using the Firebug console

We often use the method log(), which prints all the parameters passed to it, and sometimes dir(), which enumerates the object passed to it and prints all properties. Here's an example usage:

```
console.log("test", 1, {}, [1,2,3]);
console.dir({one: 1, two: {three: 3}});
```

When you type in the console, you don't have to use console.log(); you can simply omit it. To avoid clutter, some code snippets skip it, too, and assume you're testing the code in the console:

```
window.name === window['name']; // true
```

This is as if we used the following:

```
console.log(window.name === window['name']);
```

and it printed true in the console.

CHAPTER 2

Essentials

This chapter discusses essential best practices, patterns, and habits for writing high-quality JavaScript code, such as avoiding globals, using single `var` declarations, pre-caching `length` in loops, following coding conventions, and more. The chapter also includes some habits not necessarily related to the code itself, but more about the overall code creation process, including writing API documentation, conducting peer reviews, and running JSLint. These habits and best practices can help you write better, more understandable, and maintainable code—code to be proud of (and be able to figure out) when revisiting it months and years down the road.

Writing Maintainable Code

Software bugs are costly to fix. And their cost increases over time, especially if the bugs creep into the publicly released product. It's best if you can fix a bug right away, as soon you find it; this is when the problem your code solves is still fresh in your head. Otherwise you move on to other tasks and forget all about that particular code. Revisiting the code after some time has passed requires:

- Time to relearn and understand the problem
- Time to understand the code that is supposed to solve the problem

Another problem, specific to bigger projects or companies, is that the person who eventually fixes the bug is not the same person who created the bug (and also not the same person who found the bug). It's therefore critical to reduce the time it takes to understand code, either written by yourself some time ago or written by another developer in the team. It's critical to both the bottom line (business revenue) and the developer's happiness, because we would all rather develop something new and exciting instead of spending hours and days maintaining old legacy code.

Another fact of life related to software development in general is that usually more time is spent *reading* code than *writing* it. In times when you're focused and deep into a problem, you can sit down and in one afternoon create a considerable amount of code.

The code will probably work then and there, but as the application matures, many other things happen that require your code to be reviewed, revised, and tweaked. For example:

- Bugs are uncovered.
- New features are added to the application.
- The application needs to work in new environments (for example, new browsers appear on the market).
- The code gets repurposed.
- The code gets completely rewritten from scratch or ported to another architecture or even another language.

As a result of the changes, the few man-hours spent writing the code initially end up in man-weeks spent reading it. That's why creating maintainable code is critical to the success of an application.

Maintainable code means code that:

- Is readable
- Is consistent
- Is predictable
- Looks as if it was written by the same person
- Is documented

The rest of this chapter addresses these points when it comes to writing JavaScript.

Minimizing Globals

JavaScript uses functions to manage scope. A variable declared inside of a function is *local* to that function and not available outside the function. On the other hand, *global* variables are those declared outside of any function or simply used without being declared.

Every JavaScript environment has a *global object* accessible when you use this outside of any function. Every global variable you create becomes a property of the global object. In browsers, for convenience, there is an additional property of the global object called window that (usually) points to the global object itself. The following code snippet shows how to create and access a global variable in a browser environment:

```
myglobal = "hello"; // antipattern
console.log(myglobal); // "hello"
console.log(window.myglobal); // "hello"
console.log(window["myglobal"]); // "hello"
console.log(this.myglobal); // "hello"
```

The Problem with Globals

The problem with global variables is that they are shared among all the code in your JavaScript application or web page. They live in the same global *namespace* and there is always a chance of naming collisions—when two separate parts of an application define global variables with the same name but with different purposes.

It's also common for web pages to include code not written by the developers of the page, for example:

- A third-party JavaScript library
- Scripts from an advertising partner
- Code from a third-party user tracking and analytics script
- Different kinds of widgets, badges, and buttons

Let's say that one of the third-party scripts defines a global variable, called, for example, `result`. Then later in one of your functions you define another global variable called `result`. The outcome of that is the last `result` variable overwrites the previous ones, and the third-party script may just stop working.

Therefore it's important to be a good neighbor to the other scripts that may be in the same page and use as few global variables as possible. Later in the book you learn about strategies to minimize the number of globals, such as the namespacing pattern or the self-executing immediate functions, but the most important pattern for having fewer globals is to always use `var` to declare variables.

It is surprisingly easy to create globals involuntarily because of two JavaScript features. First, you can use variables without even declaring them. And second, JavaScript has the notion of *implied globals*, meaning that any variable you don't declare becomes a property of the global object (and is accessible just like a properly declared global variable). Consider the following example:

```
function sum(x, y) {
    // antipattern: implied global
    result = x + y;
    return result;
}
```

In this code, `result` is used without being declared. The code works fine, but after calling the function you end up with one more variable `result` in the global namespace that can be a source of problems.

The rule of thumb is to always declare variables with `var`, as demonstrated in the improved version of the `sum()` function:

```
function sum(x, y) {
    var result = x + y;
    return result;
}
```

Another antipattern that creates implied globals is to chain assignments as part of a var declaration. In the following snippet, a is local but b becomes global, which is probably not what you meant to do:

```
// antipattern, do not use
function foo() {
    var a = b = 0;

    // ...
}
```

If you're wondering why that happens, it's because of the right-to-left evaluation. First, the expression b = 0 is evaluated and in this case b is not declared. The return value of this expression is 0, and it's assigned to the new local variable declared with var a. In other words, it's as if you've typed:

```
var a = (b = 0);
```

If you've already declared the variables, chaining assignments is fine and doesn't create unexpected globals. Example:

```
function foo() {
    var a, b;
    // ...
    a = b = 0; // both local
}
```

 Yet another reason to avoid globals is portability. If you want your code to run in different environments (hosts), it's dangerous to use globals because you can accidentally overwrite a host object that doesn't exist in your original environment (so you thought the name was safe to use) but which does in some of the others.

Side Effects When Forgetting var

There's one slight difference between implied globals and explicitly defined ones—the difference is in the ability to undefine these variables using the delete operator:

- Globals created with var (those created in the program outside of any function) cannot be deleted.
- Implied globals created without var (regardless if created inside functions) can be deleted.

This shows that implied globals are technically not real variables, but they are properties of the global object. Properties can be deleted with the delete operator whereas variables cannot:

```
// define three globals
var global_var = 1;
global_novar = 2; // antipattern
(function () {
```

```
    global_fromfunc = 3; // antipattern
}());

// attempt to delete
delete global_var; // false
delete global_novar; // true
delete global_fromfunc; // true

// test the deletion
typeof global_var; // "number"
typeof global_novar; // "undefined"
typeof global_fromfunc; // "undefined"
```

In ES5 strict mode, assignments to undeclared variables (such as the two antipatterns in the preceding snippet) will throw an error.

Access to the Global Object

In the browsers, the global object is accessible from any part of the code via the `window` property (unless you've done something special and unexpected such as declaring a local variable named `window`). But in other environments this convenience property may be called something else (or even not available to the programmer). If you need to access the global object without hard-coding the identifier `window`, you can do the following from any level of nested function scope:

```
var global = (function () {
    return this;
}());
```

This way you can always get the global object, because inside functions that were invoked as functions (that is, not as constructors with `new`) `this` should always point to the global object. This is actually no longer the case in ECMAScript 5 in strict mode, so you have to adopt a different pattern when your code is in strict mode. For example, if you're developing a library, you can wrap your library code in an immediate function (discussed in Chapter 4) and then from the global scope, pass a reference to `this` as a parameter to your immediate function.

Single var Pattern

Using a single `var` statement at the top of your functions is a useful pattern to adopt. It has the following benefits:

- Provides a single place to look for all the local variables needed by the function
- Prevents logical errors when a variable is used before it's defined (see "Hoisting: A Problem with Scattered vars" on page 14)
- Helps you remember to declare variables and therefore minimize globals
- Is less code (to type and to transfer over the wire)

The single var pattern looks like this:

```
function func() {
    var a = 1,
        b = 2,
        sum = a + b,
        myobject = {},
        i,
        j;

    // function body...

}
```

You use one var statement and declare multiple variables delimited by commas. It's a good practice to also *initialize* the variable with an initial value at the time you declare it. This can prevent logical errors (all uninitialized and declared variables are initialized with the value undefined) and also improve the code readability. When you look at the code later, you can get an idea about the intended use of a variable based on its initial value—for example, was it supposed to be an object or an integer?

You can also do some actual work at the time of the declaration, like the case with sum = a + b in the preceding code. Another example is when working with DOM (Document Object Model) references. You can assign DOM references to local variables together with the single declaration, as the following code demonstrates:

```
function updateElement() {
    var el = document.getElementById("result"),
        style = el.style;

    // do something with el and style...

}
```

Hoisting: A Problem with Scattered vars

JavaScript enables you to have multiple var statements anywhere in a function, and they all act as if the variables were declared at the top of the function. This behavior is known as *hoisting*. This can lead to logical errors when you use a variable and then you declare it further in the function. For JavaScript, as long as a variable is in the same scope (same function), it's considered declared, even when it's used before the var declaration. Take a look at this example:

```
// antipattern
myname = "global"; // global variable
function func() {
    alert(myname); // "undefined"
    var myname = "local";
    alert(myname); // "local"
}
func();
```

In this example, you might expect that the first alert() will prompt "global" and the second will prompt "local." It's a reasonable expectation because, at the time of the first alert, myname was not declared and therefore the function should probably "see" the global myname. But that's not how it works. The first alert will say "undefined" because myname is considered declared as a local variable to the function. (Although the declaration comes after.) All the variable declarations get hoisted to the top of the function. Therefore to avoid this type of confusion, it's best to declare upfront all variables you intend to use.

The preceding code snippet will behave as if it were implemented like so:

```
myname = "global"; // global variable
function func() {
    var myname; // same as -> var myname = undefined;
    alert(myname); // "undefined"
    myname = "local";
    alert(myname); // "local"
}
func();
```

 For completeness, let's mention that actually at the implementation level things are a little more complex. There are two stages of the code handling, where variables, function declarations, and formal parameters are created at the first stage, which is the stage of parsing and entering the context. In the second stage, the stage of runtime code execution, function expressions and unqualified identifiers (undeclared variables) are created. But for practical purposes, we can adopt the concept of *hoisting*, which is actually not defined by ECMAScript standard but is commonly used to describe the behavior.

for Loops

In for loops you iterate over arrays or array-like objects such as arguments and HTMLCollection objects. The usual for loop pattern looks like the following:

```
// sub-optimal loop
for (var i = 0; i < myarray.length; i++) {
    // do something with myarray[i]
}
```

A problem with this pattern is that the length of the array is accessed on every loop iteration. This can slow down your code, especially when myarray is not an array but an HTMLCollection object.

HTMLCollections are objects returned by DOM methods such as:

- document.getElementsByName()
- document.getElementsByClassName()
- document.getElementsByTagName()

There are also a number of other `HTMLCollections`, which were introduced before the DOM standard and are still in use today. There include (among others):

`document.images`
> All IMG elements on the page

`document.links`
> All A elements

`document.forms`
> All forms

`document.forms[0].elements`
> All fields in the first form on the page

The trouble with collections is that they are live queries against the underlying document (the HTML page). This means that every time you access any collection's `length`, you're querying the live DOM, and DOM operations are expensive in general.

That's why a better pattern for `for` loops is to cache the length of the array (or collection) you're iterating over, as shown in the following example:

```
for (var i = 0, max = myarray.length; i < max; i++) {
    // do something with myarray[i]
}
```

This way you retrieve the value of `length` only once and use it during the whole loop.

Caching the length when iterating over `HTMLCollections` is faster across all browsers—anywhere between two times faster (Safari 3) and 190 times (IE7). (For more details, see *High Performance JavaScript* by Nicholas Zakas [O'Reilly].)

Note that when you explicitly intend to modify the collection in the loop (for example, by adding more DOM elements), you'd probably like the `length` to be updated and not constant.

Following the single `var` pattern, you can also take the `var` out of the loop and make the loop like:

```
function looper() {
    var i = 0,
        max,
        myarray = [];

    // ...

    for (i = 0, max = myarray.length; i < max; i++) {
        // do something with myarray[i]
    }
}
```

This pattern has the benefit of consistency because you stick to the single `var` pattern. A drawback is that it makes it a little harder to copy and paste whole loops while refactoring code. For example, if you're copying the loop from one function to another, you have to make sure you also carry over i and max into the new function (and probably delete them from the original function if they are no longer needed there).

One last tweak to the loop would be to substitute i++ with either one of these expressions:

```
i = i + 1
i += 1
```

JSLint prompts you to do it; the reason being that ++ and -- promote "excessive trickiness." If you disagree with this, you can set the JSLint option plusplus to false. (It's true by default.) Later in the book, the last pattern is used: i += 1.

Two variations of the for pattern introduce some micro-optimizations because they:

- Use one less variable (no max)
- Count down to 0, which is usually faster because it's more efficient to compare to 0 than to the length of the array or to anything other than 0

The first modified pattern is:

```
var i, myarray = [];

for (i = myarray.length; i--;) {
    // do something with myarray[i]
}
```

And the second uses a while loop:

```
var myarray = [],
    i = myarray.length;

while (i--) {
    // do something with myarray[i]
}
```

These are micro-optimizations and will only be noticed in performance-critical operations. Additionally, JSLint will complain about the use of i--.

for-in Loops

for-in loops should be used to iterate over nonarray objects. Looping with for-in is also called *enumeration*.

Technically, you can also use for-in to loop over arrays (because in JavaScript arrays are objects), but it's not recommended. It may lead to logical errors if the array object has already been augmented with custom functionality. Additionally, the order (the sequence) of listing the properties is not guaranteed in a for-in. So it's preferable to use normal for loops with arrays and for-in loops for objects.

It's important to use the method hasOwnProperty() when iterating over object properties to filter out properties that come down the prototype chain.

Consider the following example:

```javascript
// the object
var man = {
    hands: 2,
    legs: 2,
    heads: 1
};

// somewhere else in the code
// a method was added to all objects
if (typeof Object.prototype.clone === "undefined") {
    Object.prototype.clone = function () {};
}
```

In this example we have a simple object called man defined with an object literal. Somewhere before or after man was defined, the Object prototype was augmented with a useful method called clone(). The prototype chain is live, which means all objects automatically get access to the new method. To avoid having the clone() method show up when enumerating man, you need to call hasOwnProperty() to filter out the prototype properties. Failing to do the filtering can result in the function clone() showing up, which is undesired behavior in mostly all scenarios:

```javascript
// 1.
// for-in loop
for (var i in man) {
    if (man.hasOwnProperty(i)) { // filter
        console.log(i, ":", man[i]);
    }
}
/*
result in the console
hands : 2
legs : 2
heads : 1
*/


// 2.
// antipattern:
// for-in loop without checking hasOwnProperty()
for (var i in man) {
    console.log(i, ":", man[i]);
}
/*
result in the console
hands : 2
legs : 2
heads : 1
clone: function()
*/
```

Another pattern for using hasOwnProperty() is to call that method off of the Object.prototype, like so:

```
for (var i in man) {
    if (Object.prototype.hasOwnProperty.call(man, i)) { // filter
        console.log(i, ":", man[i]);
    }
}
```

The benefit is that you can avoid naming collisions in case the man object has redefined hasOwnProperty. Also to avoid the long property lookups all the way to Object, you can use a local variable to "cache" it:

```
var i,
    hasOwn = Object.prototype.hasOwnProperty;
for (i in man) {
    if (hasOwn.call(man, i)) { // filter
        console.log(i, ":", man[i]);
    }
}
```

 Strictly speaking, not using hasOwnProperty() is not an error. Depending on the task and the confidence you have in the code, you may skip it and slightly speed up the loops. But when you're not sure about the contents of the object (and its prototype chain), you're safer just adding the hasOwnProperty() check.

A formatting variation (which doesn't pass JSLint) skips a curly brace and puts the if on the same line. The benefit is that the loop statement reads more like a complete thought ("for each element that has an own property X, do something with X"). Also there's less indentation before you get to the main purpose of the loop:

```
// Warning: doesn't pass JSLint
var i,
    hasOwn = Object.prototype.hasOwnProperty;
for (i in man) if (hasOwn.call(man, i)) { // filter
    console.log(i, ":", man[i]);
}
```

(Not) Augmenting Built-in Prototypes

Augmenting the prototype property of constructor functions is a powerful way to add functionality, but it can be too powerful sometimes.

It's tempting to augment prototypes of built-in constructors such as Object(), Array(), or Function(), but it can seriously hurt maintainability, because it will make your code less predictable. Other developers using your code will probably expect the built-in JavaScript methods to work consistently and will not expect your additions.

Additionally, properties you add to the prototype may show up in loops that don't use `hasOwnProperty()`, so they can create confusion.

Therefore it's best if you don't augment built-in prototypes. You can make an exception of the rule only when all these conditions are met:

1. It's expected that future ECMAScript versions or JavaScript implementations will implement this functionality as a built-in method consistently. For example, you can add methods described in ECMAScript 5 while waiting for the browsers to catch up. In this case you're just defining the useful methods ahead of time.

2. You check if your custom property or method doesn't exist already—maybe already implemented somewhere else in the code or already part of the JavaScript engine of one of the browsers you support.

3. You clearly document and communicate the change with the team.

If these three conditions are met, you can proceed with the custom addition to the prototype, following this pattern:

```
if (typeof Object.prototype.myMethod !== "function") {
    Object.protoype.myMethod = function () {
        // implementation...
    };
}
```

switch Pattern

You can improve the readability and robustness of your `switch` statements by following this pattern:

```
var inspect_me = 0,
    result = '';

switch (inspect_me) {
case 0:
    result = "zero";
    break;
case 1:
    result = "one";
    break;
default:
    result = "unknown";
}
```

The style conventions followed in this simple example are:

- Aligning each `case` with `switch` (an exception to the curly braces indentation rule).
- Indenting the code within each `case`.
- Ending each `case` with a clear `break;`.

- Avoiding fall-throughs (when you omit the break intentionally). If you're abso-lutely convinced that a fall-through is the best approach, make sure you document such cases, because they might look like errors to the readers of your code.

- Ending the switch with a default: to make sure there's always a sane result even if none of the cases matched.

Avoiding Implied Typecasting

JavaScript implicitly typecasts variables when you compare them. That's why compar-isons such as false == 0 or "" == 0 return true.

To avoid confusion caused by the implied typecasting, always use the === and !== operators that check both the values and the type of the expressions you compare:

```
var zero = 0;
if (zero === false) {
    // not executing because zero is 0, not false
}

// antipattern
if (zero == false) {
    // this block is executed...
}
```

There's another school of thought that subscribes to the opinion that it's redundant to use === when == is sufficient. For example, when you use typeof you know it returns a string, so there's no reason to use strict equality. However, JSLint requires strict equal-ity; it does make the code look consistent and reduces the mental effort when reading code. ("Is this == intentional or an omission?")

Avoiding eval()

If you spot the use of eval() in your code, remember the mantra "eval() is evil." This function takes an arbitrary string and executes it as JavaScript code. When the code in question is known beforehand (not determined at runtime), there's no reason to use eval(). If the code is dynamically generated at runtime, there's often a better way to achieve the goal without eval(). For example, just using square bracket notation to access dynamic properties is better and simpler:

```
// antipattern
var property = "name";
alert(eval("obj." + property));

// preferred
var property = "name";
alert(obj[property]);
```

Using eval() also has security implications, because you might be executing code (for example coming from the network) that has been tampered with. This is a common antipattern when dealing with a JSON response from an Ajax request. In those cases it's better to use the browsers' built-in methods to parse the JSON response to make sure it's safe and valid. For browsers that don't support `JSON.parse()` natively, you can use a library from JSON.org.

It's also important to remember that passing strings to `setInterval()`, `setTimeout()`, and the `Function()` constructor is, for the most part, similar to using `eval()` and therefore should be avoided. Behind the scenes, JavaScript still has to evaluate and execute the string you pass as programming code:

```
// antipatterns
setTimeout("myFunc()", 1000);
setTimeout("myFunc(1, 2, 3)", 1000);

// preferred
setTimeout(myFunc, 1000);
setTimeout(function () {
    myFunc(1, 2, 3);
}, 1000);
```

Using the `new Function()` constructor is similar to `eval()` and should be approached with care. It could be a powerful construct but is often misused. If you absolutely must use `eval()`, you can consider using `new Function()` instead. There is a small potential benefit because the code evaluated in `new Function()` will be running in a local function scope, so any variables defined with `var` in the code being evaluated will not become globals automatically. Another way to prevent automatic globals is to wrap the `eval()` call into an immediate function (more about immediate functions in Chapter 4).

Consider the following example. Here only `un` remains as a global variable polluting the namespace:

```
console.log(typeof un);    // "undefined"
console.log(typeof deux);  // "undefined"
console.log(typeof trois); // "undefined"

var jsstring = "var un = 1; console.log(un);";
eval(jsstring); // logs "1"

jsstring = "var deux = 2; console.log(deux);";
new Function(jsstring)(); // logs "2"

jsstring = "var trois = 3; console.log(trois);";
(function () {
    eval(jsstring);
}()); // logs "3"

console.log(typeof un);    // "number"
console.log(typeof deux);  // "undefined"
console.log(typeof trois); // "undefined"
```

Another difference between `eval()` and the `Function` constructor is that `eval()` can interfere with the scope chain whereas `Function` is much more sandboxed. No matter where you execute `Function`, it sees only the global scope. So it can do less local variable pollution. In the following example, eval() can access and modify a variable in its outer scope, whereas Function cannot (also note that using Function or new Function is identical):

```
(function () {
    var local = 1;
    eval("local = 3; console.log(local)"); // logs 3
    console.log(local); // logs 3
}());


(function () {
    var local = 1;
    Function("console.log(typeof local);")(); // logs undefined
}());
```

Number Conversions with parseInt()

Using parseInt() you can get a numeric value from a string. The function accepts a second radix parameter, which is often omitted but shouldn't be. The problems occur when the string to parse starts with 0: for example, a part of a date entered into a form field. Strings that start with 0 are treated as octal numbers (base 8) in ECMAScript 3; however, this has changed in ES5. To avoid inconsistency and unexpected results, always specify the radix parameter:

```
var month = "06",
    year = "09";
month = parseInt(month, 10);
year = parseInt(year, 10);
```

In this example, if you omit the radix parameter like parseInt(year), the returned value will be 0, because "09" assumes octal number (as if you did parseInt(year, 8)) and 09 is not a valid digit in base 8.

Alternative ways to convert a string to a number include:

```
+"08" // result is 8
Number("08") // 8
```

These are often faster than parseInt(), because parseInt(), as the name suggests, parses and doesn't simply convert. But if you're expecting input such as "08 hello", parseInt() will return a number, whereas the others will fail with NaN.

Coding Conventions

It's important to establish and follow coding conventions—they make your code consistent, *predictable*, and much easier to read and understand. A new developer joining the team can read through the conventions and be productive much sooner, understanding the code written by any other team member.

Many flamewars have been fought in meetings and on mailing lists over specific aspects of certain coding conventions (for example, the code indentation—tabs or spaces?). So if you're the one suggesting the adoption of conventions in your organization, be prepared to face resistance and hear different but equally strong opinions. Remember that it's much more important to establish and consistently follow a convention, any convention, than what the exact details of that convention will be.

Indentation

Code without indentation is impossible to read. The only thing worse is code with inconsistent indentation, because it looks like it's following a convention, but it may have confusing surprises along the way. It's important to standardize the use of indentation.

Some developers prefer indentation with tabs, because anyone can tweak their editor to display the tabs with the individually preferred number of spaces. Some prefer spaces—usually four. It doesn't matter as long as everyone in the team follows the same convention. This book, for example, uses four-space indentation, which is also the default in JSLint.

And what should you indent? The rule is simple—anything within curly braces. This means the bodies of functions, loops (do, while, for, for-in), ifs, switches, and object properties in the object literal notation. The following code shows some examples of using indentation:

```
function outer(a, b) {
    var c = 1,
        d = 2,
        inner;
    if (a > b) {
        inner = function () {
            return {
                r: c - d
            };
        };
    } else {
        inner = function () {
            return {
                r: c + d
            };
        };
    }
    return inner;
}
```

Curly Braces

Curly braces should always be used, even in cases when they are optional. Technically, if you have only one statement in an if or a for, curly braces are not required, but you

---

should always use them anyway. It makes the code more consistent and easier to update.

Imagine you have a `for` loop with one statement only. You could omit the braces and there will be no syntax error:

```
// bad practice
for (var i = 0; i < 10; i += 1)
    alert(i);
```

But what if, later on, you add another line in the body of the loop?

```
// bad practice
for (var i = 0; i < 10; i += 1)
    alert(i);
    alert(i + " is " + (i % 2 ? "odd" : "even"));
```

The second `alert` is outside the loop although the indentation may trick you. The best thing to do in the long run is to always use the braces, even for one-line blocks:

```
// better
for (var i = 0; i < 10; i += 1) {
    alert(i);
}
```

Similarly for `if` conditions:

```
// bad
if (true)
    alert(1);
else
    alert(2);
```

```
// better
if (true) {
    alert(1);
} else {
    alert(2);
}
```

Opening Brace Location

Developers also tend to have preferences about where the opening curly brace should be—on the same line or on the following line?

```
if (true) {
    alert("It's TRUE!");
}
```

Or:

```
if (true)
{
    alert("It's TRUE!");
}
```

In this specific example, it's a matter of preference, but there are cases in which the program might behave differently depending on where the brace is. This is because of the *semicolon insertion mechanism*—JavaScript is not picky when you choose not to end your lines properly with a semicolon and adds it for you. This behavior can cause troubles when a function returns an object literal and the opening brace is on the next line:

```
// warning: unexpected return value
function func() {
    return
    {
        name: "Batman"
    };
}
```

If you expect this function to return an object with a `name` property, you'll be surprised. Because of the implied semicolons, the function returns `undefined`. The preceding code is equivalent to this one:

```
// warning: unexpected return value
function func() {
    return undefined;
    // unreachable code follows...
    {
        name: "Batman"
    };
}
```

In conclusion, always use curly braces and always put the opening one on the same line as the previous statement:

```
function func() {
    return {
        name: "Batman"
    };
}
```

 A note on semicolons: Just like with the curly braces, you should always use semicolons, even when they are *implied* by the JavaScript parsers. This not only promotes discipline and a more rigorous approach to the code but also helps resolve ambiguities, as the previous example showed.

White Space

The use of white space can also contribute to improved readability and consistency of the code. In written English sentences you use intervals after commas and periods. In JavaScript you follow the same logic and add intervals after list-like expressions (equivalent to commas) and end-of-statements (equivalent to completing a "thought").

Good places to use a white space include:

- After the semicolons that separate the parts of a for loop: for example, `for (var i = 0; i < 10; i += 1) {...}`
- Initializing multiple variables (i and `max`) in a for loop: `for (var i = 0, max = 10; i < max; i += 1) {...}`
- After the commas that delimit array items: `var a = [1, 2, 3];`
- After commas in object properties and after colons that divide property names and their values: `var o = {a: 1, b: 2};`
- Delimiting function arguments: `myFunc(a, b, c)`
- Before the curly braces in function declarations: `function myFunc() {}`
- After `function` in anonymous function expressions: `var myFunc = function () {};`

Another good use for white space is to separate all operators and their operands with spaces, which basically means use a space before and after +, -, *, =, <, >, <=, >=, ===, !==, &&, ||, +=, and so on:

```
// generous and consistent spacing
// makes the code easier to read
// allowing it to "breathe"
var d = 0,
    a = b + 1;
if (a && b && c) {
    d = a % c;
    a += d;
}

// antipattern
// missing or inconsistent spaces
// make the code confusing
var d= 0,
    a =b+1;
if (a&& b&&c) {
d=a %c;
    a+= d;
}
```

And a final note about white space—curly braces spacing. It's good to use a space:

- Before opening curly braces ({) in functions, `if-else` cases, loops, and object literals
- Between the closing curly brace (}) and `else` or `while`

A case against liberal use of white space might be that it could increase the file size, but minification (discussed later in the chapter) takes care of this issue.

 An often-overlooked aspect of code readability is the use of vertical white space. You can use blank lines to separate units of code, just as paragraphs are used in literature to separate ideas.

Naming Conventions

Another way to make your code more predictable and maintainable is to adopt naming conventions. That means choosing names for your variables and functions in a consistent manner.

Below are some naming convention suggestions that you can adopt as-is or tweak to your liking. Again, having a convention and following it consistently is much more important than what that convention actually is.

Capitalizing Constructors

JavaScript doesn't have classes but has constructor functions invoked with new:

```
var adam = new Person();
```

Because constructors are still just functions, it helps if you can tell, just by looking at a function name, whether it was supposed to behave as a constructor or as a normal function.

Naming constructors with a capital first letter provides that hint. Using lowercase for functions and methods indicates that they are not supposed to be called with new:

```
function MyConstructor() {...}
function myFunction() {...}
```

In the next chapter there are some patterns that enable you to programmatically force your constructors to behave like constructors, but simply following the naming convention is helpful in itself, at least for programmers reading the source code.

Separating Words

When you have multiple words in a variable or a function name, it's a good idea to follow a convention as to how the words will be separated. A common convention is to use the so-called *camel case*. Following the camel case convention, you type the words in lowercase, only capitalizing the first letter in each word.

For your constructors, you can use *upper camel case*, as in MyConstructor(), and for function and method names, you can use *lower camel case*, as in myFunction(), calculateArea() and getFirstName().

And what about variables that are not functions? Developers commonly use lower camel case for variable names, but another good idea is to use all lowercase words delimited by an underscore: for example, first_name, favorite_bands, and old_company_name. This notation helps you visually distinguish between functions and all other identifiers—primitives and objects.

ECMAScript uses camel case for both methods and properties, although the multiword property names are rare (`lastIndex` and `ignoreCase` properties of regular expression objects).

Other Naming Patterns

Sometimes developers use a naming convention to make up or substitute language features.

For example, there is no standard way to define constants in JavaScript yet (although there are some built-in such as `Number.MAX_VALUE` and, additionally, a `const` is expected in ECMAScript 6), so developers have adopted the convention of using all-caps for naming variables that shouldn't change values during the life of the program, like:

```
// precious constants, please don't touch
var PI = 3.14,
    MAX_WIDTH = 800;
```

There's another convention that competes for the use of all caps: using capital letters for names of global variables. Naming globals with all caps can reinforce the practice of minimizing their number and can make them easily distinguishable.

Another case of using a convention to mimic functionality is the private members convention. Although you can implement true privacy in JavaScript, sometimes developers find it easier to just use an underscore prefix to denote a private method or property. Consider the following example:

```
var person = {
    getName: function () {
        return this._getFirst() + ' ' + this._getLast();
    },
    _getFirst: function () {
        // ...
    },
    _getLast: function () {
        // ...
    }
};
```

In this example `getName()` is meant to be a public method, part of the stable API, whereas `_getFirst()` and `_getLast()` are meant to be private. They are still normal public methods, but using the underscore prefix warns the users of the `person` object that these methods are not guaranteed to work in the next release and shouldn't be used directly. Note that JSLint will complain about the underscore prefixes, unless you set the option `nomen: false`.

Following are some varieties to the `_private` convention:

- Using a trailing underscore to mean private, as in `name_` and `getElements_()`
- Using one underscore prefix for `_protected` properties and two for `__private` properties

- In Firefox some internal properties not technically part of the language are available, and they are named with a two underscores prefix and a two underscore suffix, such as __proto__ and __parent__

Writing Comments

You have to comment your code, even if it's unlikely that someone other than you will ever touch it. Often when you're deep into a problem you think it's obvious what the code does, but when you come back to the code after a week, you have a hard time remembering how it worked exactly.

You shouldn't go overboard commenting the obvious: every single variable or every single line. But you usually need to document all functions, their arguments and return values, and also any interesting or unusual algorithm or technique. Think of the comments as hints to the future readers of the code; the readers need to understand what your code does without reading much more than just the comments and the function and property names. When you have, for example, five or six lines of code performing a specific task, the reader can skip the code details if you provide a one-line description describing the *purpose* of the code and why it's there. There's no hard and fast rule or ratio of comments-to-code; some pieces of code (think regular expressions) may actually require more comments than code.

 The most important habit, yet hardest to follow, is to keep the comments up to date, because outdated comments can mislead and be much worse than no comments at all.

And as you'll see in the next section, comments can help you auto-generate documentation.

Writing API Docs

Most developers consider writing documentation a boring and unrewarding task. But that doesn't have to be the case. API documentation can be auto-generated from comments in the code. This way you can have the documentation written without actually writing it. Most programmers find this idea fascinating, because auto-generating a readable reference from specific keywords and specially formatted "commands" looks much like actual programming.

Traditionally API docs come from the Java world, where a utility called javadoc is distributed together with the Java SDK (Software Developer Kit). But the same idea has been ported to many other languages. And for JavaScript there are two excellent tools, both free and open source: the JSDoc Toolkit (*http://code.google.com/p/jsdoc-toolkit/*) and YUIDoc (*http://yuilibrary.com/projects/yuidoc*).

The process of generating API documentation includes:

- Writing specially formatted code blocks
- Running a tool to parse the code and the comments
- Publishing the results of the tool, which are most often HTML pages

The special syntax you need to learn consists of a dozen or so *tags*, which look like this:

```
/**
 * @tag value
 */
```

For example, say you have a function called `reverse()` that flips a string around. It takes a string parameter and at the end returns another string. Documenting it could look like this:

```
/**
 * Reverse a string
 *
 * @param  {String} input String to reverse
 * @return {String} The reversed string
 */
var reverse = function (input) {
    // ...
    return output;
};
```

You can see that `@param` is the tag for input parameters and `@return` is the tag used to document return values. The documentation tool parses these tags and produces a set of nicely formatted HTML documents at the end.

YUIDoc Example

YUIDoc was originally created with the purpose of documenting the YUI (Yahoo! User Interface) library, but it can be used for any project. It has some conventions that you should follow to make the best use of the tool, for example, the notion of modules and classes. (Although there's no such thing as classes in JavaScript.)

Let's see a complete example of generating documentation using YUIDoc.

Figure 2-1 shows a preview of the nicely formatted documentation you'll get at the end. You can actually tweak the HTML template to make it even nicer and more customized to your project needs, look, and feel.

For a live demo of the example, visit *http://jspatterns.com/book/2/*.

In this example, the whole application consists of one file only (`app.js`) with only one module (`myapp`) in it. You'll learn more about modules in the following chapters, but for now, just think of the module as a comment tag you need to make YUIDoc work.

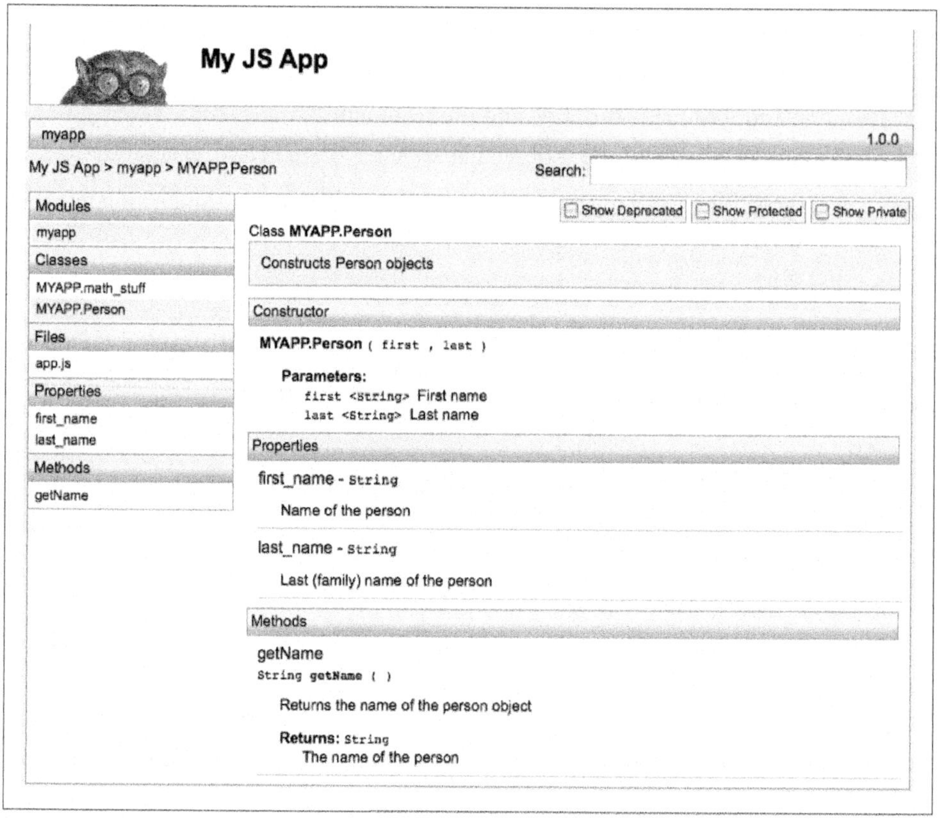

My JS App

myapp   1.0.0

My JS App > myapp > MYAPP.Person   Search:

Modules	
myapp	

☐ Show Deprecated ☐ Show Protected ☐ Show Private

Class MYAPP.Person

Classes

MYAPP.math_stuff
MYAPP.Person

Constructs Person objects

Files

app.js

Constructor

Properties

first_name
last_name

MYAPP.Person (first , last)

Parameters:
first <String> First name
last <String> Last name

Methods

getName

Properties

first_name - String

    Name of the person

last_name - String

    Last (family) name of the person

Methods

getName
String getName ( )

    Returns the name of the person object

    Returns: String
        The name of the person

Figure 2-1. Documentation generated by YUIDoc

The contents of app.js starts like this:

```
/**
 * My JavaScript application
 *
 * @module myapp
 */
```

Then you define a blank object to use as a namespace:

```
var MYAPP = {};
```

And then you define an object math_stuff that has two methods: sum() and multi():

```
/**
 * A math utility
 * @namespace MYAPP
 * @class math_stuff
 */
MYAPP.math_stuff = {

    /**
     * Sums two numbers
```

```
    *
    * @method sum
    * @param  {Number} a First number
    * @param  {Number} b The second number
    * @return {Number} The sum of the two inputs
    */
   sum: function (a, b) {
       return a + b;
   },

   /**
    * Multiplies two numbers
    *
    * @method multi
    * @param  {Number} a First number
    * @param  {Number} b The second number
    * @return {Number} The two inputs multiplied
    */
   multi: function (a, b) {
       return a * b;
   }
};
```

And that completes the first "class." Note the highlighted tags:

@namespace
> The global reference that contains your object.

@class
> A misnomer (no classes in JavaScript) that is used to mean either an object or a constructor function.

@method
> Defines a method in an object and specifies the method name.

@param
> Lists the arguments that a function takes. The types of the parameters are in curly braces, followed by the parameter name and its description.

@return
> Like @param, only it describes the value returned by the method and has no name.

For the second "class," let's use a constructor function and add a method to its prototype, just to get a feeling for how the documentation system works with the different ways to create objects:

```
/**
 * Constructs Person objects
 * @class Person
 * @constructor
 * @namespace MYAPP
 * @param {String} first First name
 * @param {String} last Last name
 */
MYAPP.Person = function (first, last) {
```

```
    /**
     * Name of the person
     * @property first_name
     * @type String
     */
    this.first_name = first;
    /**
     * Last (family) name of the person
     * @property last_name
     * @type String
     */
    this.last_name  = last;

};

/**
 * Returns the name of the person object
 *
 * @method getName
 * @return {String} The name of the person
 */
MYAPP.Person.prototype.getName = function () {
    return this.first_name + ' ' + this.last_name;
};
```

In Figure 2-1 you can see what the generated documentation for this `Person` constructor looks like. The highlighted parts here are:

- `@constructor` hints that this "class" is actually a constructor function
- `@property` and `@type` describe properties of an object

The YUIDoc system is language-agnostic and only parses the comment blocks, not the JavaScript code. The drawback is that you have to state the names of properties, parameters, and methods in the comments, for example, `@property first_name`. The benefit is that when you're comfortable with it, you can use the same system to document code in any language.

Writing to Be Read

Writing the comments for the API doc blocks is not only a lazy way to provide reference documentation, but it also serves another purpose—improving code quality by making you revisit your code.

Any writer or editor will tell you that editing is important: probably the most important step in producing a good book or article. Getting it down on paper is only the first step, the first draft. The draft communicates some information to the reader but probably not in the most clear, structured, or easy-to-follow manner.

The same applies to writing code. When you sit down and solve a problem, that solution is merely a first draft. It produces the desired output, but does it do so in the best way? Is it easy to read, understand, maintain, and update? When you revisit your code, ideally after some time has passed, you will most certainly see areas for improvement—ways to make the code easier to follow, remove some inefficiencies, and so on. That's essentially editing, and it can help enormously toward your goal of creating high-quality code. But more often than not, we work under tight deadlines ("here's the problem, the solution is due yesterday") and there's no time for editing. That's why writing API docs is an editing opportunity.

Often when you write doc comment blocks, you revisit the problem. Sometimes revisiting makes it clear that, for example, this third parameter to a method is actually more often needed than the second, and the second will almost always default to true, so it makes sense to tweak the method's interface and swap them.

Writing to be read means writing code, or even just the API, with the idea that someone else will read it. This fact alone will make you edit and think of better ways to solve the problem you have at hand.

Talking about first drafts, there's also the idea of "plan to throw one away." It may look a little extreme at first, but it makes a lot of sense, especially when you have a mission-critical project at hand (and human lives depend on it). The idea is that the first solution you come up with should be thrown away and then you start from scratch. The first solution may be a working solution, but it's nothing more than a draft, one example way to solve a problem. The second solution will always be better, because you now have a much deeper understanding of the problem. In the second solution, you're also not allowed to copy-paste from the first one, which helps prevent you from taking shortcuts or settling for the nonperfect solution.

Peer Reviews

Another way to make your code better is to have it peer reviewed. Peer reviews could be formal and standardized, even aided by specialized tools, and this is a great way to make the reviews a streamlined part of the development process. But not having the time to research and adopt review tools shouldn't be in the way. You can simply ask the developer next to you to take a look at your code or you can walk her through it.

Again, as with writing API docs or any type of documentation, peer reviews help you write clearer code, simply because you know someone else will need to read and understand what you're doing.

Peer reviews are a good practice not only because the resulting code is better, but also because both reviewer and creator share and exchange knowledge and learn from each other's experience and individual approaches.

If you're a one-person shop and don't have any peers to review your code, that also shouldn't be an obstacle. You can always open-source at least a part of the code or simply blog about an interesting piece of it and this way have the world be your reviewer.

Another good practice is to have your source control system (CVS, Subversion, Git) send an email notification to the team any time someone checks in code. Most of these emails will be unread, but every once in a while a spontaneous peer review might happen when someone decides to take a break from their work and take a look at the code you just checked in.

Minify...In Production

Minification is the process of eliminating white space, comments, and other nonessential parts of the JavaScript code to decrease the size of the JavaScript files that need to be transferred from the server to the browser. This is usually done by a tool (a minifier) such as the Yahoo! YUICompressor or Google's Closure Compiler and helps speed up the page loading time. It is important to minify the production-ready scripts because this results in significant savings, often cutting the size in half.

Here's what a sample of a minified code looks like (this is part of YUI2 Library's Event utility):

```
YAHOO.util.CustomEvent=function(D,C,B,A){this.type=D;this.scope=C||window;this.silent
=B;this.signature=A||YAHOO.util.CustomEvent.LIST;this.subscribers=[];if(!this.silent)
{}var E="_YUICEOnSubscribe";if(D!==E){this.subscribeEvent=new
YAHOO.util.CustomEvent(E,this,true);}...
```

In addition to stripping white space, new lines, and comments, minifiers also rename variables to shorter names (but only when it's safe to do so), such as the parameters D, C, B, A in the preceding code. Minifiers can rename only local variables because renaming globals might break the code. This is why it's a good practice to use local variables whenever possible. If you use a global variable, such as a DOM reference, more than once or twice in a function, it's a good practice to assign it to a local variable. This will speed up the lookups when resolving a variable name, and so the code will be faster during runtime in addition to minifying better and being downloaded faster.

As a side note, Google Closure Compiler will also attempt to minify global variables as well (in "advanced" mode), which is risky and requires some attention and discipline on your end to take advantage of that extra minification.

Minifying your production code is important because it helps the page performance, but you should leave this job to the minifier. It's a mistake to attempt to write pre-minified code. You should always use descriptive variable names, consistent white space and indentation, comments, and so on. The code you write will be read (by humans), so make it easy for the maintainer to understand it quickly and let the minifier (the machine) take care of reducing the file sizes.

Run JSLint

JSLint was already introduced in the previous chapter and is also mentioned on numerous occasions in this chapter. At this point you're probably convinced that it's a good programming pattern to run JSLint on your code.

What does JSLint look for? It looks for violations of some of the patterns discussed in this chapter (single `var` pattern, radix for `parseInt()`, always using curly braces) and many other violations including:

- Unreachable code
- Using variables before they are defined
- Unsafe UTF characters
- Using `void`, `with`, or `eval`
- Improperly escaped characters in regular expressions

JSLint is written in JavaScript (and would most probably pass a JSLint check); the good news is that it's available as a web-based tool and as downloadable code for many platforms and JavaScript interpreters. You can download it and run it locally on any platform using WSH (Windows Scripting Host, part of all Windows systems), JSC (JavaScriptCore, part of Mac OSX), or Rhino (JavaScript interpreter by Mozilla).

It's a great idea to download JSLint and integrate it with your text editor so that you adopt the habit of running it every time you save a file. (Making a keyboard shortcut for it can also help.)

Summary

In this chapter we looked at what it means to write maintainable code—a topic that is important not only for the success of a software project but also to the sanity and well-being of the developers and those around them. Then we talked about some of the essential best practices and patterns including:

- Reducing the number of globals, ideally to one per application
- Using a single `var` per function, which helps keep an eye on all variables in a single spot and prevents surprises caused by the variable hoisting behavior
- `for` loops, `for-in` loops, `switches`, "eval() is evil," not augmenting built-in prototypes
- Following coding conventions (consistent white space, indentation, using curly braces and semicolons even when they are optional) and naming conventions (for constructors, functions, and variables)

The chapter also discussed some additional practices, not related to the code, but to the programming process in general—writing comments, creating generated API documentation, conducting peer reviews, not attempting to write minified code at the expense of readability, and always checking your code with JSLint.

CHAPTER 3

Literals and Constructors

Literal notation patterns available in JavaScript enable more concise, more expressive, and less error-prone object definitions. This chapter discusses literals such as object, array, and regular expression literals and why they are preferable to using equivalent built-in constructor functions, such as `Object()` and `Array()`. The JSON format is introduced to demonstrate how array and object literals are used to define a data transfer format. The chapter also discusses custom constructors and ways to enforce `new` to make sure constructors behave as intended.

To extend the main message of the chapter (which is to avoid constructors and use literals instead), there's a discussion of the built-in wrapper constructors `Number()`, `String()`, and `Boolean()` and how they compare to the primitive number, string, and boolean values. Finally there's a quick note on the use of the different built-in `Error()` constructors.

Object Literal

When you think about objects in JavaScript, simply think about hash tables of key-value pairs (similar to what are called "associative arrays" in other languages). The values can be primitives or other objects; in both cases they are called *properties*. The values can also be functions, in which case they are called *methods*.

The custom objects you create in JavaScript (in other words, the *user-defined* native objects) are mutable at any time. Many of the properties of the *built-in* native objects are also mutable. You can start with a blank object and add functionality to it as you go. The *object literal notation* is ideal for this type of on-demand object creation.

Consider the following example:

```
// start with an empty object
var dog = {};

// add one property
dog.name = "Benji";
```

```
// now add a method
dog.getName = function () {
    return dog.name;
};
```

In the preceding example, you begin with a clean slate—a blank object. Then you add a property and a method to it. At any time in the life of the program you can:

- Change the values of properties and methods, for example:

```
dog.getName = function () {
    // redefine the method to return
    // a hardcoded value
    return "Fido";
};
```

- Remove properties/methods completely:

```
delete dog.name;
```

- Add more properties and methods:

```
dog.say = function () {
    return "Woof!";
};
dog.fleas = true;
```

You are not required to start with an empty object. The object literal pattern enables you to add functionality to the object at the time of creation, as the next example demonstrates.

```
var dog = {
    name: "Benji",
    getName: function () {
        return this.name;
    }
};
```

 You'll see "blank object" and "empty object" in a few places throughout this book. It's important to understand that this is for simplicity and there's no such thing as an empty object in JavaScript. Even the simplest {} object already has properties and methods inherited from Object.prototype. By "empty" we'll understand an object that has no own properties other than the inherited ones.

The Object Literal Syntax

If you're not used to the object literal notation, it may look a little odd at the beginning, but the more you use it, the more you'll love it. In essence, the syntax rules are:

- Wrap the object in curly braces ({ and }).
- Comma-delimit the properties and methods inside the object. A trailing comma after the last name-value pair is allowed but produces errors in IE, so don't use it.

- Separate property names and property values with a colon.
- When you assign the object to a variable, don't forget the semicolon after the closing }.

Objects from a Constructor

There are no classes in JavaScript and this allows for great flexibility, because you don't have to know anything about your object in advance; you don't need a class "blueprint." But JavaScript also has constructor functions, which use syntax similar to the class-based object creation in Java or other languages.

You can create objects using your own constructor functions or using some of the built-in constructors such as `Object()`, `Date()`, `String()` and so on.

Here's an example showing two equivalent ways to create two identical objects:

```
// one way -- using a literal
var car = {goes: "far"};

// another way -- using a built-in constructor
// warning: this is an antipattern
var car = new Object();
car.goes = "far";
```

As you can see from this example, an obvious benefit of the literal notation is that it's shorter to type. Another reason why *the literal is the preferred pattern for object creation* is that it emphasizes that objects are simply mutable hashes and not something that needs to be baked from a "recipe" (from a class).

Another reason for using literals as opposed to the `Object` constructor is that there is no scope resolution. Because it's possible that you have created a local constructor with the same name, the interpreter needs to look up the scope chain from the place you are calling `Object()` all the way up until it finds the global `Object` constructor.

Object Constructor Catch

You have no reason to use the `new Object()` constructor when you can use an object literal, but you might be inheriting legacy code written by others, so you should be aware of one "feature" of this constructor (or yet another reason not to use it). The feature in question is that the `Object()` constructor accepts a parameter and, depending on the value passed, it may decide to delegate the object creation to another built-in constructor and return a different object than you expect.

Following are a few examples of passing a number, a string, and a boolean value to `new Object()`; the result is that you get objects created with a different constructor:

```
// Warning: antipatterns ahead

// an empty object
var o = new Object();
```

```
console.log(o.constructor === Object); // true

// a number object
var o = new Object(1);
console.log(o.constructor === Number); // true
console.log(o.toFixed(2)); // "1.00"

// a string object
var o = new Object("I am a string");
console.log(o.constructor === String); // true
// normal objects don't have a substring()
// method but string objects do
console.log(typeof o.substring); // "function"

// a boolean object
var o = new Object(true);
console.log(o.constructor === Boolean); // true
```

This behavior of the `Object()` constructor can lead to unexpected results when the value you pass to it is dynamic and not known until runtime. Again, in conclusion, don't use new `Object()`; use the simpler and reliable object literal instead.

Custom Constructor Functions

In addition to the object literal pattern and the built-in constructor functions, you can create objects using your own custom constructor functions, as the following example demonstrates:

```
var adam = new Person("Adam");
adam.say(); // "I am Adam"
```

This new pattern looks very much like creating an object in Java using a class called Person. The syntax is similar, but actually in JavaScript there are no classes and Person is just a function.

Here's how the Person constructor function could be defined.

```
var Person = function (name) {
    this.name = name;
    this.say = function () {
        return "I am " + this.name;
    };
};
```

When you invoke the constructor function with new, the following happens inside the function:

- An empty object is created and referenced by this variable, inheriting the prototype of the function.
- Properties and methods are added to the object referenced by this.
- The newly created object referenced by this is returned at the end implicitly (if no other object was returned explicitly).

It's as if something like this happens behind the scenes:

```
var Person = function (name) {

    // create a new object
    // using the object literal
    // var this = {};

    // add properties and methods
    this.name = name;
    this.say = function () {
        return "I am " + this.name;
    };

    // return this;
};
```

For simplicity in this example, the say() method was added to this. The result is that any time you call new Person() a new function is created in memory. This is obviously inefficient, because the say() method doesn't change from one instance to the next. The better option is to add the method to the prototype of Person:

```
Person.prototype.say = function () {
    return "I am " + this.name;
};
```

We'll talk more about prototypes and inheritance in the chapters to come, but just remember that reusable members, such as methods, should go to the prototype.

There is one more thing that will become clear later in the book, but it is worth mentioning here for the sake of completeness. We said that inside of the constructor something like this happens behind the scenes:

```
// var this = {};
```

That's not the whole truth, because the "empty" object is not actually empty; it has inherited from the Person's prototype. So it's more like:

```
// var this = Object.create(Person.prototype);
```

We'll discuss what Object.create() means later in the book.

Constructor's Return Values

When invoked with new, a constructor function always returns an object; by default it's the object referred to by this. If you don't add any properties to this inside of your constructor, an "empty" object is returned ("empty" aside from inheriting from the constructor's prototype).

Constructors implicitly return this, even when you don't have a return statement in the function. But you can return any other object of your choosing. In the next example, a new object referenced by that is created and returned.

```
var Objectmaker = function () {

    // this `name` property will be ignored
    // because the constructor
    // decides to return another object instead
    this.name = "This is it";

    // creating and returning a new object
    var that = {};
    that.name = "And that's that";
    return that;
};

// test
var o = new Objectmaker();
console.log(o.name); // "And that's that"
```

As can you see, you have the freedom to return any object in your constructors, as long
as it's an object. Attempting to return something that's not an object (like a string or a
boolean false, for example) will not cause an error but will simply be ignored, and the
object referenced by this will be returned instead.

Patterns for Enforcing new

As mentioned already, constructors are still just functions but invoked with new. What
happens if you forget new when you invoke a constructor? This is not going to cause
syntax or runtime errors but might lead to logical errors and unexpected behavior.
That's because when you forget new, this inside the constructor will point to the global
object. (In browsers this will point to window.)

When your constructor has something like this.member and you invoke the constructor
without new, you're actually creating a new property of the global object called
member and accessible through window.member or simply member. This behavior is highly
undesirable, because you know you should always strive for keeping the global namespace clean.

```
// constructor
function Waffle() {
    this.tastes = "yummy";
}

// a new object
var good_morning = new Waffle();
console.log(typeof good_morning); // "object"
console.log(good_morning.tastes); // "yummy"

// antipattern:
// forgotten `new`
var good_morning = Waffle();
console.log(typeof good_morning); // "undefined"
console.log(window.tastes); // "yummy"
```

This undesired behavior is addressed in ECMAScript 5, and in strict mode this will no longer point to the global object. If ES5 is not available, there's still something you can do to make sure that a constructor function always behaves like one even if called without new.

Naming Convention

The simplest alternative is to use a naming convention, as discussed in the previous chapter, where you uppercase the first letter in constructor names (MyConstructor) and lowercase it in "normal" functions and methods (myFunction).

Using that

Following a naming convention can certainly help, but it merely suggests and doesn't enforce the correct behavior. Here's a pattern that helps you make sure your constructor always behaves as a constructor. Instead of adding all members to this, you add them to that and then return that.

```
function Waffle() {
    var that = {};
    that.tastes = "yummy";
    return that;
}
```

For simpler objects, you don't even need a local variable such as that; you can simply return an object from a literal like so:

```
function Waffle() {
    return {
        tastes: "yummy"
    };
}
```

Using any of the implementations above Waffle() always returns an object, regardless of how it's called:

```
var first = new Waffle(),
    second = Waffle();
console.log(first.tastes); // "yummy"
console.log(second.tastes); // "yummy"
```

The problem with this pattern is that the link to the prototype is lost, so any members you add to the Waffle() prototype will not be available to the objects.

 Note that the variable name that is just a convention; it's not a part of the language. You can use any name, where other common variable names include self and me.

Self-Invoking Constructor

To address the drawback of the previous pattern and have prototype properties available to the instance objects, consider the following approach. In the constructor you check whether this is an instance of your constructor, and if not, the constructor invokes itself again, this time properly with new:

```
function Waffle() {

    if (!(this instanceof Waffle)) {
        return new Waffle();
    }

    this.tastes = "yummy";

}
Waffle.prototype.wantAnother = true;


// testing invocations
var first = new Waffle(),
    second = Waffle();

console.log(first.tastes); // "yummy"
console.log(second.tastes); // "yummy"

console.log(first.wantAnother); // true
console.log(second.wantAnother); // true
```

Another general-purpose way to check the instance is to compare with arguments.callee instead of hard-coding the constructor name.

```
if (!(this instanceof arguments.callee)) {
    return new arguments.callee();
}
```

This pattern uses the fact that inside every function, an object called arguments is created containing all parameters passed to the function when it was invoked. And arguments has a property called callee, which points back to the function that was called. Be aware that arguments.callee is not allowed in ES5's strict mode, so it's best if you limit its future use and also remove any instances should you find them in existing code.

Array Literal

Arrays in JavaScript, as most other things in the language, are objects. They can be created with the built-in constructor function Array(), but they also have a literal notation and, just like the object literal, the array literal notation is simpler and preferred.

Here's how you can create two arrays with the same elements in two different ways—using the Array() constructor and using the literal pattern.

```
// array of three elements
// warning: antipattern
var a = new Array("itsy", "bitsy", "spider");

// the exact same array
var a = ["itsy", "bitsy", "spider"];

console.log(typeof a); // "object", because arrays are objects
console.log(a.constructor === Array); // true
```

Array Literal Syntax

There's not much to the array literal notation: it's just a comma-delimited list of elements and the whole list is wrapped in square brackets. You can assign any type of value to the array elements, including objects or other arrays.

The array literal syntax is simple, straightforward, and elegant. After all, an array is just a zero-indexed list of values. There's no need to complicate things (and write more code) by including a constructor and using the new operator.

Array Constructor Curiousness

One more reason to stay away from new Array() is to avoid a possible trap that this constructor has in store for you.

When you pass a single number to the Array() constructor, it doesn't become the value of the first array element. It sets the length of the array instead. This means that new Array(3) creates an array with length of 3, but no actual elements. If you try to access any of the elements, you get the value undefined because the elements don't exist. The following code example shows the different behavior when you use the literal and the constructor with a single value.

```
// an array of one element
var a = [3];
console.log(a.length); // 1
console.log(a[0]); // 3

// an array of three elements
var a = new Array(3);
console.log(a.length); // 3
console.log(typeof a[0]); // "undefined"
```

Although this behavior might be a little unexpected, it gets worse when you pass a floating point number to new Array() as opposed to an integer. This results in an error because the floating point is not a valid value for the array's length:

```
// using array literal
var a = [3.14];
console.log(a[0]); // 3.14
```

```
var a = new Array(3.14); // RangeError: invalid array length
console.log(typeof a); // "undefined"
```

To avoid potential errors when creating dynamic arrays at runtime, it's much safer to stick with the array literal notation.

 There are some clever uses of the Array() constructor though, for example, for repeating strings. The following snippet returns a string with 255 white spaces (why not 256, I'll leave the curious reader to think about):

```
var white = new Array(256).join(' ');
```

Check for Array-ness

Using the typeof operator with array operands returns "object."

```
console.log(typeof [1, 2]); // "object"
```

Although this behavior makes sense (arrays are objects), it's not too helpful. Often you need to know if a value actually is an array. Sometimes you can see code checking for the presence of length property or some array method such as slice() to determine "array-ness." But these checks are not robust because there's no reason why a nonarray object shouldn't have properties and methods with the same names. Also people sometimes use instanceof Array, but this check works incorrectly when used across frames in some IE versions.

ECMAScript 5 defines a new method Array.isArray(), which returns true if the argument is an array. For example:

```
Array.isArray([]); // true

// trying to fool the check
// with an array-like object
Array.isArray({
    length: 1,
    "0": 1,
    slice: function () {}
}); // false
```

If this new method is not available in your environment, you can make the check by calling the Object.prototype.toString() method. If you invoke the call() method of toString in the context of an array, it should return the string "[object Array]". If the context is an object, it should return the string "[object Object]". So you can do something like this:

```
if (typeof Array.isArray === "undefined") {
    Array.isArray = function (arg) {
        return Object.prototype.toString.call(arg) === "[object Array]";
    };
}
```

JSON

Now that you're familiar with the array and object literals previously discussed, let's take a look at JSON, which stands for JavaScript Object Notation and is a data transfer format. It's lightweight and convenient to work with in many languages, especially in JavaScript.

There's actually nothing new to learn about JSON. It's only a combination of the array and the object literal notation. Here's an example of a JSON string:

```
{"name": "value", "some": [1, 2, 3]}
```

The only syntax difference between JSON and the object literal is that property names need to be wrapped in quotes to be valid JSON. In object literals the quotes are required only when the property names are not valid identifiers, for example, they have spaces `{"first name": "Dave"}`.

In JSON strings you cannot use functions or regular expression literals.

Working with JSON

As mentioned in the previous chapter, it's not recommended to blindly evaluate any JSON string with `eval()` because of the security implications. It's best if you use the `JSON.parse()` method, which is part of the language since ES5 and is natively provided by the JavaScript engines in modern browsers. For older JavaScript engines, you can use the JSON.org library (*http://www.json.org/json2.js*) to gain access to the JSON object and its methods.

```
// an input JSON string
var jstr = '{"mykey": "my value"}';

// antipattern
var data = eval('(' + jstr + ')');

// preferred
var data = JSON.parse(jstr);

console.log(data.mykey); // "my value"
```

If you already use a JavaScript library, chances are that it comes with a utility to parse JSON, so you may not need the additional JSON.org library. For example, using YUI3, you can do:

```
// an input JSON string
var jstr = '{"mykey": "my value"}';

// parse the string and turn it into an object
// using a YUI instance
YUI().use('json-parse', function (Y) {
    var data = Y.JSON.parse(jstr);
    console.log(data.mykey); // "my value"
});
```

In jQuery, there's the parseJSON() method:

```
// an input JSON string
var jstr = '{"mykey": "my value"}';

var data = jQuery.parseJSON(jstr);
console.log(data.mykey); // "my value"
```

The opposite of JSON.parse() method is JSON.stringify(). It takes any object or array (or a primitive) and serializes it into a JSON string.

```
var dog = {
    name: "Fido",
    dob:  new Date(),
    legs: [1, 2, 3, 4]
};

var jsonstr = JSON.stringify(dog);

// jsonstr is now:
// {"name":"Fido","dob":"2010-04-11T22:36:22.436Z","legs":[1,2,3,4]}
```

Regular Expression Literal

Regular expressions in JavaScript are also objects, and you have two options to create them:

- Using the new RegExp() constructor
- Using the regular expression literal

The following sample code demonstrates two ways to create a regular expression that matches a backslash:

```
// regular expression literal
var re = /\\/gm;

// constructor
var re = new RegExp("\\\\", "gm");
```

As you can see, the regular expression literal notation is shorter and doesn't force you to think in terms of class-like constructors. Therefore it's preferable to use the literal.

Additionally, when using the RegExp() constructor, you also need to escape quotes and often you need to double-escape backslashes, as shown in the preceding snippet, where we need four backslashes to match a single one. This makes your regular expression patterns longer and harder to read and modify. Regular expressions are hard enough to begin with, and any chance to simplify them is welcome, so it's best to stick to the literal notation.

Regular Expression Literal Syntax

The regular expression literal notation uses forward slashes to wrap the regular expression pattern used for matching. Following the second slash, you can put the pattern modifiers in the form of unquoted letters:

- g—Global matching
- m—Multiline
- i—Case-insensitive matching

The pattern modifiers can appear in any order or combination:

```
var re = /pattern/gmi;
```

Using the regular expression literal helps write more concise code when calling methods such as `String.prototype.replace()` that accept regular expression objects as parameters.

```
var no_letters = "abc123XYZ".replace(/[a-z]/gi, "");
console.log(no_letters); // 123
```

One reason to use `new RegExp()` is that the pattern is not known in advance but is created as a string at runtime.

Another distinction between the regular expression literal and the constructor is that the literal creates an object only once during parse time. If you create the same regular expression in a loop, the previously created object will be returned with all its properties (such as `lastIndex`) already set from the first time. Consider the following example as an illustration of how the same object is returned twice.

```
function getRE() {
    var re = /[a-z]/;
    re.foo = "bar";
    return re;
}

var reg = getRE(),
    re2 = getRE();

console.log(reg === re2); // true
reg.foo = "baz";
console.log(re2.foo); // "baz"
```

 This behavior has changed in ES5 and the literal also creates new objects. The behavior has also been corrected in many browser environments, so it's not to be relied on.

And one last note that calling `RegExp()` without `new` (as a function, not as a constructor) behaves the same as with `new`.

Primitive Wrappers

JavaScript has five primitive value types: number, string, boolean, null, and undefined. With the exception of null and undefined, the other three have the so-called *primitive wrapper objects*. The wrapper objects can be created using the built-in constructors Number(), String(), and Boolean().

To illustrate the difference between a *primitive* number and a number *object*, consider the following example:

```
// a primitive number
var n = 100;
console.log(typeof n); // "number"

// a Number object
var nobj = new Number(100);
console.log(typeof nobj); // "object"
```

The wrapper objects have some useful properties and methods—for example, number objects have methods such as toFixed() and toExponential(). String objects have substring(), charAt(), and toLowerCase() methods (among others) and a length property. These methods are convenient and can be a good reason to decide to create an object, as opposed to using a primitive. But the methods work on primitives, too—as soon as you invoke a method, the primitive is temporarily converted to an object behind the scenes and behaves as if it were an object.

```
// a primitive string be used as an object
var s = "hello";
console.log(s.toUpperCase()); // "HELLO"

// the value itself can act as an object
"monkey".slice(3, 6);  // "key"

// same for numbers
(22 / 7).toPrecision(3); // "3.14"
```

Because primitives can act as objects as soon as you need them to, often there's no reason to use the more verbose wrapper constructors. For example, you don't have to write new String("hi"); when you can simply use "hi":

```
// avoid these:
var s = new String("my string");
var n = new Number(101);
var b = new Boolean(true);

// better and simpler:
var s = "my string";
var n = 101;
var b = true;
```

One reason to use the wrapper objects is when you want to augment the value and persist state. Because primitives are not objects, they cannot be augmented with properties.

```
// primitive string
var greet = "Hello there";

// primitive is converted to an object
// in order to use the split() method
greet.split(' ')[0]; // "Hello"

// attemting to augment a primitive is not an error
greet.smile = true;

// but it doesn't actually work
typeof greet.smile; // "undefined"
```

In the preceding snippet, greet was only temporarily converted to an object to make the property/method access work without errors. On the other hand, if greet were defined as an object using new String(), then the augmented smile property would've worked as expected. Augmenting a string, number, or boolean value is rarely used, and unless this is what you need, you probably don't need the wrapper constructors.

When used without new, wrapper constructors convert the argument passed to them to a primitive value:

```
typeof Number(1); // "number"
typeof Number("1"); // "number"
typeof Number(new Number()); // "number"
typeof String(1); // "string"
typeof Boolean(1); // "boolean"
```

Error Objects

JavaScript has a number of built-in error constructors, such as Error(), SyntaxError(), TypeError(), and others, which are used with the throw statement. The error objects created by these constructors have the following properties:

name
: The name property of the constructor function that created the object; it could be the general "Error" or a more specialized constructor such as "RangeError"

message
: The string passed to the constructor when creating the object

The error objects have other properties, such as the line number and filename where the error happened, but these extra properties are browser extensions inconsistently implemented across browsers and are therefore unreliable.

On the other hand, throw works with any object, not necessarily an object created with one of the error constructors, so you can opt in for throwing your own objects. Such error objects can have the properties "name," "message," and any other type of information you want to pass to be handled by the catch statement. You can be creative when it comes to your custom error objects and use them to restore the application state back to normal.

```
try {
    // something bad happened, throw an error
    throw {
        name: "MyErrorType", // custom error type
        message: "oops",
        extra: "This was rather embarrassing",
        remedy: genericErrorHandler // who should handle it
    };
} catch (e) {
    // inform the user
    alert(e.message); // "oops"

    // gracefully handle the error
    e.remedy(); // calls genericErrorHandler()
}
```

The error constructors invoked as functions (without new) behave the same as constructors (with new) and return the same error objects.

Summary

In this chapter you've learned about different literal patterns, which are simpler alternatives to using constructor functions. The chapter discussed:

- Object literal notation—An elegant way to create objects as comma-delimited key-value pairs, wrapped in curly brackets.
- Constructor functions—Built-in constructors (which almost always have a better and shorter literal notation) and custom constructors
- Ways to make sure custom constructors always behave as if invoked with new
- Array literal notation—Comma-delimited lists of values inside square brackets
- JSON—A data format consisting of object and array literals
- Regular expression literals
- Other built-in constructors to avoid: String(), Number(), Boolean(), and the different Error() constructors

In general, with the exception of the Date() constructor, there's rarely a need to use the other built-in constructors. The following table summarizes these constructors and their corresponding and preferred literal patterns.

Built-in constructors (avoid)	Literals and primitives (prefer)
`var o = new Object();`	`var o = {};`
`var a = new Array();`	`var a = [];`

`var re = new RegExp(`
`    "[a-z]",`
`    "g"`
`);`
	`var re = /[a-z]/g;`

`var s = new String();`	`var s = "";`
`var n = new Number();`	`var n = 0;`
`var b = new Boolean();`	`var b = false;`

`throw new Error("uh-oh");`	`throw {`
	`    name: "Error",`
	`    message: "uh-oh"`
	`};`
	
	… or
	
	`throw Error("uh-oh");`

CHAPTER 4

Functions

Mastering functions is an essential skill for the JavaScript programmer because the language has many uses for them. They perform a variety of tasks for which other languages may have special syntax.

In this chapter you will learn about the different ways to define a function in JavaScript, you will learn about function expressions and function declarations, and you will see how the local scope and the variable hoisting works. Then you will learn about a number of patterns that help your APIs (providing better interfaces to your functions), code initializations (with fewer globals), and performance (in other words—work avoidance).

Let's dive into functions, starting by first reviewing and clarifying the important basics.

Background

There are two main features of the functions in JavaScript that make them special—the first is that functions are *first-class objects* and the second is that they provide scope.

Functions are objects that:

- Can be created dynamically at runtime, during the execution of the program
- Can be assigned to variables, can have their references copied to other variables, can be augmented, and, except for a few special cases, can be deleted
- Can be passed as arguments to other functions and can also be returned by other functions
- Can have their own properties and methods

So it could happen that a function A, being an object, has properties and methods, one of which happens to be another function B. Then B can accept a function C as an argument and, when executed, can return another function D. At first sight, that's a lot of functions to keep track of. But when you're comfortable with the various applications of the functions, you get to appreciate the power, flexibility, and expressiveness that functions can offer. In general, when you think of a function in JavaScript, think of an object, with the only special feature that this object is invokable, meaning it can be executed.

The fact that functions are objects becomes obvious when you see the new Function() constructor in action:

```
// antipattern
// for demo purposes only
var add = new Function('a, b', 'return a + b');
add(1, 2); // returns 3
```

In this code, there's no doubt that add() is an object; after all it was created by a constructor. Using the Function() constructor is not a good idea though (it's as bad as eval()) because code is passed around as a string and evaluated. It's also inconvenient to write (and read) because you have to escape quotes and take extra care if you want to properly indent the code inside the function for readability.

The second important feature is that functions provide scope. In JavaScript there's no curly braces local scope; in other words, blocks don't create scope. There's only function scope. Any variable defined with var inside of a function is a local variable, invisible outside the function. Saying that curly braces don't provide local scope means that if you define a variable with var inside of an if condition or inside of a for or a while loop, that doesn't mean the variable is local to that if or for. It's only local to the wrapping function, and if there's no wrapping function, it becomes a global variable. As discussed in Chapter 2, minimizing the number of globals is a good habit, so functions are indispensable when it comes to keeping the variable scope under control.

Disambiguation of Terminology

Let's take a moment to discuss the terminology surrounding the code used to define a function, because using accurate and agreed-upon names is just as important as the code when talking about patterns.

Consider the following snippet:

```
// named function expression
var add = function add(a, b) {
    return a + b;
};
```

The preceding code shows a function, which uses a named function expression.

If you skip the name (the second add in the example) in the function expression, you get an unnamed function expression, also known as simply as function expression or most commonly as an anonymous function. An example is:

```
// function expression, a.k.a. anonymous function
var add = function (a, b) {
    return a + b;
};
```

So the broader term is "function expression" and the "named function expression" is a specific case of a function expression, which happens to define the optional name.

When you omit the second add and end up with an unnamed function expression, this won't affect the definition and the consecutive invocations of the function. The only difference is that the name property of the function object will be a blank string. The name property is an extension of the language (it's not part of the ECMA standard) but widely available in many environments. If you keep the second add, then the property add.name will contain the string "add." The name property is useful when using debuggers, such as Firebug, or when calling the same function recursively from itself; otherwise you can just skip it.

Finally, you have *function declarations.* They look the most similar to functions used in other languages:

```
function foo() {
    // function body goes here
}
```

In terms of syntax, named function expressions and function declarations look similar, especially if you don't assign the result of the function expression to a variable (as we'll see in the callback pattern further in the chapter). Sometimes there's no other way to tell the difference between a function declaration and a named function expression other than looking at the context in which the function occurs, as you'll see in the next section.

There's syntax difference between the two in the trailing semicolon. The semicolon is not needed in function declarations but is required in function expressions, and you should always use it even though the automatic semicolon insertion mechanism might do it for you.

> The term *function literal* is also commonly used. It may mean either a function expression or a named function expression. Because of this ambiguity, it's probably better if we don't use it.

Declarations Versus Expressions: Names and Hoisting

So what should you use—function declarations or function expressions? In cases in which syntactically you cannot use a declaration, this dilemma is solved for you. Examples include passing a function object as a parameter or defining methods in object literals:

```
// this is a function expression,
// pased as an argument to the function `callMe`
callMe(function () {
    // I am an unnamed function expression
    // also known as an anonymous function
});
```

```
// this is a named function expression
callMe(function me() {
    // I am a named function expression
    // and my name is "me"
});

// another function expression
var myobject = {
    say: function () {
        // I am a function expression
    }
};
```

Function declarations can only appear in "program code," meaning inside of the bodies of other functions or in the global space. Their definitions cannot be assigned to variables or properties, or appear in function invocations as parameters. Here's an example of the allowed usage of function declarations, where all the functions foo(), bar(), and local() are defined using the function declaration pattern:

```
// global scope
function foo() {}

function local() {
    // local scope
    function bar() {}
    return bar;
}
```

Function's name Property

Another thing to consider when choosing a function definition pattern is the availability of the read-only name property. Again, this property is not standard but available in many environments. In function declarations and named function expressions, the name property is defined. In anonymous function expressions, it depends on the implementation; it could be undefined (IE) or defined with an empty string (Firefox, WebKit):

```
function foo() {} // declaration
var bar = function () {}; // expression
var baz = function baz() {}; // named expression

foo.name; // "foo"
bar.name; // ""
baz.name; // "baz"
```

The name property is useful when debugging code in Firebug or other debuggers. When the debugger needs to show you an error in a function, it can check for the presence of the name property and use it as an indicator. The name property is also used to call the same function recursively from within itself. If you were not interested in these two cases, then an unnamed function expression would be easier and less verbose.

The case against function declarations and the reason to prefer function expressions is that the expressions highlight that functions are objects like all other objects and not some special language construct.

It's technically possible to use a named function expression and assign it to a variable with a different name, for example:

```
var foo = function bar() {};
```

However, the behavior of this usage is not properly implemented in some browsers (IE), so it's not recommended to use this pattern.

Function Hoisting

From the previous discussion you may conclude that the behavior of function declarations is pretty much equivalent to a *named* function expression. That's not exactly true, and a difference lies in the hoisting behavior.

The term *hoisting* is not defined in ECMAScript, but it's common and a good way to describe the behavior.

As you know, all variables, no matter where in the function body they are declared, get hoisted to the top of the function behind the scenes. The same applies for functions because they are just objects assigned to variables. The only "gotcha" is that when using a function declaration, the definition of the function also gets hoisted, not only its declaration. Consider this snippet:

```
// antipattern
// for illustration only

// global functions
function foo() {
    alert('global foo');
}
function bar() {
    alert('global bar');
}

function hoistMe() {

    console.log(typeof foo); // "function"
    console.log(typeof bar); // "undefined"

    foo(); // "local foo"
    bar(); // TypeError: bar is not a function

    // function declaration:
    // variable 'foo' and its implementation both get hoisted
```

```
function foo() {
    alert('local foo');
}

// function expression:
// only variable 'bar' gets hoisted
// not the implementation
var bar = function () {
    alert('local bar');
};

}
hoistMe();
```

In this example you see that, just like with normal variables, the mere presence of foo and bar anywhere in the hoistMe() function moves them to the top, overwriting the global foo and bar. The difference is that local foo()'s *definition* is hoisted to the top and works fine; although it's defined later. The definition of bar() is not hoisted, only its declaration. That's why until the code execution reaches bar()'s definition, it's undefined and not usable as a function (while still preventing the global bar() from being "seen" in the scope chain).

Now that the required background and terminology surrounding functions is out of the way, let's see some of the good patterns related to functions that JavaScript has to offer, starting with the callback pattern. Again, it's important to remember the two special features of the functions in JavaScript:

- They are objects.
- They provide local scope.

Callback Pattern

Functions are objects, which means that they can be passed as arguments to other functions. When you pass the function introduceBugs() as a parameter to the function writeCode(), then at some point writeCode() is likely to execute (or call) introduceBugs(). In this case introduceBugs() is called a *callback function* or simply a *callback*:

```
function writeCode(callback) {
    // do something...
    callback();
    // ...
}

function introduceBugs() {
    // ... make bugs
}

writeCode(introduceBugs);
```

Note how `introduceBugs()` is passed as an argument to `writeCode()` without the parentheses. Parentheses execute a function whereas in this case we want to pass only a reference to the function and let `writeCode()` execute it (in other words, call it back) when appropriate.

A Callback Example

Let's take an example and start without a callback first and then refactor later. Imagine you have a general-purpose function that does some complicated work and returns a large data set as a result. This generic function could be called, for example, `findNodes()`, and its task would be to crawl the DOM tree of a page and return an array of page elements that are interesting to you:

```
var findNodes = function () {
    var i = 100000, // big, heavy loop
        nodes = [], // stores the result
        found; // the next node found
    while (i) {
        i -= 1;
        // complex logic here...
        nodes.push(found);
    }
    return nodes;
};
```

It's a good idea to keep this function generic and have it simply return an array of DOM nodes, without doing anything with the actual elements. The logic of modifying nodes could be in a different function, for example a function called `hide()` which, as the name suggests, hides the nodes from the page:

```
var hide = function (nodes) {
    var i = 0, max = nodes.length;
    for (; i < max; i += 1) {
        nodes[i].style.display = "none";
    }
};

// executing the functions
hide(findNodes());
```

This implementation is inefficient, because `hide()` has to loop again through the array of nodes returned by `findNodes()`. It would be more efficient if you could avoid this loop and hide the nodes as soon as you select them in `findNodes()`. But if you implement the hiding logic in `findNodes()`, it will no longer be a generic function because of the *coupling* of the retrieval and modification logic. Enter the callback pattern—you pass your node hiding logic as a callback function and delegate its execution:

```
// refactored findNodes() to accept a callback
var findNodes = function (callback) {
    var i = 100000,
        nodes = [],
        found;
```

```
// check if callback is callable
if (typeof callback !== "function") {
    callback = false;
}

while (i) {
    i -= 1;

    // complex logic here...

    // now callback:
    if (callback) {
        callback(found);
    }

    nodes.push(found);
}
return nodes;
};
```

The implementation is straightforward; the only additional task that findNodes() performs is checking if an optional callback has been provided, and if so, executing it. The
callback is optional, so the refactored findNodes() can still be used as before and won't
break the old code that relies on the old API.

The hide() implementation will be much simpler now because it doesn't need to loop
through nodes:

```
// a callback function
var hide = function (node) {
    node.style.display = "none";
};

// find the nodes and hide them as you go
findNodes(hide);
```

The callback can be an existing function as shown in the preceding code, or it can be
an anonymous function, which you create as you call the main function. For example,
here's how you can show nodes using the same generic findNodes() function:

```
// passing an anonymous callback
findNodes(function (node) {
    node.style.display = "block";
});
```

Callbacks and Scope

In the previous examples, the part where the callback is executed was like so:

```
callback(parameters);
```

Although this is simple and will be good enough in many cases, there are often scenarios
where the callback is not a one-off anonymous function or a global function, but it's a

---

method of an object. If the callback method uses this to refer to the object it belongs to, this can cause unexpected behavior.

Imagine the callback is the function paint(), which is a method of the object called myapp:

```
var myapp = {};
myapp.color = "green";
myapp.paint = function (node) {
    node.style.color = this.color;
};
```

The function findNodes() does something like this:

```
var findNodes = function (callback) {
    // ...
    if (typeof callback === "function") {
        callback(found);
    }
    // ...
};
```

If you call findNodes(myapp.paint), it won't work as expected, because this.color will not be defined. The object this will refer to the global object because findNodes() is invoked as a function, not as a method. If findNodes() was defined as a method of an object called dom (like dom.findNodes()), then this inside of the callback would refer to dom instead of the expected myapp.

The solution to this problem is to pass the callback function and in addition pass the object this callback belongs to:

```
findNodes(myapp.paint, myapp);
```

Then you also need to modify findNodes() to bind that object you pass:

```
var findNodes = function (callback, callback_obj) {
    //...
    if (typeof callback === "function") {
        callback.call(callback_obj, found);
    }
    // ...
};
```

There will be more on the topics of binding and using call() and apply() in future chapters.

Another option for passing an object and a method to be used as a callback is to pass the method as a string, so you don't repeat the object twice. In other words:

```
findNodes(myapp.paint, myapp);
```

can become:

```
findNodes("paint", myapp);
```

Then findNodes() would do something along these lines:

```
var findNodes = function (callback, callback_obj) {

    if (typeof callback === "string") {
        callback = callback_obj[callback];
    }

    //...
    if (typeof callback === "function") {
        callback.call(callback_obj, found);
    }
    // ...
};
```

Asynchronous Event Listeners

The callback pattern has many everyday uses; for example, when you attach an event listener to an element on a page, you're actually providing a pointer to a callback function that will be called when the event occurs. Here's a simple example of how console.log() is passed as a callback when listening to the document's click event:

```
document.addEventListener("click", console.log, false);
```

Most of the client-side browser programming is event-driven. When the page is done loading, it fires a load event. Then the user interacts with the page and causes various events to fire, such as click, keypress, mouseover, mousemove, and so on. JavaScript is especially suited for event-driven programming, because of the callback pattern, which enables your programs to work *asynchronously,* in other words, out of order.

"Don't call us, we'll call you" is a famous phrase in Hollywood, where many candidates audition for the same role in a movie. It would be impossible for the casting crew to answer phone calls from all the candidates all the time. In the asynchronous event-driven JavaScript, there is a similar phenomenon. Only instead of giving your phone number, you provide a callback function to be called when the time is right. You may even provide more callbacks than needed, because certain events may never happen. For example, if the user never clicks "Buy now!" then your function that validates the credit card number format will never be called back.

Timeouts

Another example of the callback pattern in the wild is when you use the timeout methods provided by the browser's window object: setTimeout() and setInterval(). These methods also accept and execute callbacks:

```
var thePlotThickens = function () {
    console.log('500ms later...');
};
setTimeout(thePlotThickens, 500);
```

Note again how the function thePlotThickens is passed as a variable, without parentheses, because you don't want it executed right away, but simply want to point to it for later use by `setTimeout()`. Passing the string `"thePlotThickens()"` instead of a function pointer is a common antipattern similar to `eval()`.

Callbacks in Libraries

The callback is a simple and powerful pattern, which can come in handy when you're designing a library. The code that goes into a software library should be as generic and reusable as possible, and the callbacks can help with this generalization. You don't need to predict and implement every feature you can think of, because it will bloat the library, and most of the users will never need a big chunk of those features. Instead, you focus on core functionality and provide "hooks" in the form of callbacks, which will allow the library methods to be easily built upon, extended, and customized.

Returning Functions

Functions are objects, so they can be used as return values. This means that a function doesn't need to return some sort of data value or array of data as a result of its execution. A function can return another more specialized function, or it can create another function on-demand, depending on some inputs.

Here's a simple example: A function does some work, probably some one-off initialization, and then works on its return value. The returned value happens to be another function, which can also be executed:

```
var setup = function () {
    alert(1);
    return function () {
        alert(2);
    };
};

// using the setup function
var my = setup(); // alerts 1
my(); // alerts 2
```

Because `setup()` wraps the returned function, it creates a closure, and you can use this closure to store some private data, which is accessible by the returned function but not to the outside code. An example would be a counter that gives you an incremented value every time you call it:

```
var setup = function () {
    var count = 0;
    return function () {
        return (count += 1);
    };
};

// usage
var next = setup();
next(); // returns 1
```

```
next(); // 2
next(); // 3
```

Self-Defining Functions

Functions can be defined dynamically and can be assigned to variables. If you create a new function and assign it to the same variable that already holds another function, you're overwriting the old function with the new one. In a way, you're recycling the old function pointer to point to a new function. And all this can happen inside the body of the old function. In this case the function overwrites and redefines itself with a new implementation. This probably sounds more complicated than it is; let's take a look at a simple example:

```
var scareMe = function () {
    alert("Boo!");
    scareMe = function () {
        alert("Double boo!");
    };
};

// using the self-defining function
scareMe(); // Boo!
scareMe(); // Double boo!
```

This pattern is useful when your function has some initial preparatory work to do and it needs to do it only once. Because there's no reason to do repeating work when it can be avoided, a portion of the function may no longer be required. In such cases, the self-defining function can update its own implementation.

Using this pattern can obviously help with the performance of your application, because your redefined function simply does less work.

 Another name for this pattern is "lazy function definition," because the function is not properly defined until the first time it's used and it is being lazy afterwards, doing less work.

A drawback of the pattern is that any properties you've previously added to the original function will be lost when it redefines itself. Also if the function is used with a different name, for example, assigned to a different variable or used as a method of an object, then the redefinition part will never happen and the original function body will be executed.

Let's see an example where the scareMe() function is used in a way that a first-class object would be used:

1. A new property is added.
2. The function object is assigned to a new variable.

---

3. The function is also used as a method.

Consider the following snippet:

```
// 1. adding a new property
scareMe.property = "properly";

// 2. assigning to a different name
var prank = scareMe;

// 3. using as a method
var spooky = {
    boo: scareMe
};

// calling with a new name
prank(); // "Boo!"
prank(); // "Boo!"
console.log(prank.property); // "properly"

// calling as a method
spooky.boo(); // "Boo!"
spooky.boo(); // "Boo!"
console.log(spooky.boo.property);  // "properly"

// using the self-defined function
scareMe(); // Double boo!
scareMe(); // Double boo!
console.log(scareMe.property); // undefined
```

As you can see, the self-definition didn't happen as you probably expected when the function was assigned to a new variable. Every time prank() was called, it alerted "Boo!" At the same time it overwrote the global scareMe() function, but prank() itself kept seeing the old definition including the property property. The same happened when the function was used as the boo() method of the spooky object. All these invocations kept rewriting the global scareMe() pointer so that when it was eventually called, it had the updated body alerting "Double boo" right from the first time. It was also no longer able to see scareMe.property.

Immediate Functions

The immediate function pattern is a syntax that enables you to execute a function as soon as it is defined. Here's an example:

```
(function () {
    alert('watch out!');
}());
```

This pattern is in essence just a function expression (either named or anonymous), which is executed right after its creation. The term *immediate function* is not defined in the ECMAScript standard, but it's short and helps describe and discuss the pattern.

The pattern consists of the following parts:

- You define a function using a function expression. (A function declaration won't work.)
- You add a set of parentheses at the end, which causes the function to be executed immediately.
- You wrap the whole function in parentheses (required only if you don't assign the function to a variable).

The following alternative syntax is also common (note the placement of the closing parentheses), but JSLint prefers the first one:

```
(function () {
    alert('watch out!');
})();
```

This pattern is useful because it provides a *scope sandbox* for your initialization code. Think about the following common scenario: Your code has to perform some setup tasks when the page loads, such as attaching event handlers, creating objects, and so on. All this work needs to be done only once, so there's no reason to create a reusable named function. But the code also requires some temporary variables, which you won't need after the initialization phase is complete. It would be a bad idea to create all those variables as globals. That's why you need an immediate function—to wrap all your code in its local scope and not leak any variables in the global scope:

```
(function () {

    var days = ['Sun', 'Mon', 'Tue', 'Wed', 'Thu', 'Fri', 'Sat'],
        today = new Date(),
        msg = 'Today is ' + days[today.getDay()] + ', ' + today.getDate();

    alert(msg);

}()); // "Today is Fri, 13"
```

If this code weren't wrapped in an immediate function, then the variables `days`, `today`, and `msg` would all be global variables, leftovers from the initialization code.

Parameters of an Immediate Function

You can also pass arguments to immediate functions, as the following example demonstrates:

```
// prints:
// I met Joe Black on Fri Aug 13 2010 23:26:59 GMT-0800 (PST)

(function (who, when) {

    console.log("I met " + who + " on " + when);

}("Joe Black", new Date()));
```

Commonly, the global object is passed as an argument to the immediate function so that it's accessible inside of the function without having to use `window`: this way makes the code more interoperable in environments outside the browser:

```
(function (global) {

    // access the global object via `global`

}(this));
```

Note that in general you shouldn't pass too many parameters to an immediate function, because it could quickly become a burden to constantly scroll to the top and to the bottom of the function to understand how it works.

Returned Values from Immediate Functions

Just like any other function, an immediate function can return values and these return values can be assigned to variables:

```
var result = (function () {
    return 2 + 2;
}());
```

Another way to achieve the same is to omit the parentheses that wrap the function, because they are not required when you assign the return value of an immediate function to a variable. Omitting the first set of parentheses gives you the following:

```
var result = function () {
    return 2 + 2;
}();
```

This syntax is simpler, but it may look a bit misleading. Failing to notice the () at the end of the function, someone reading the code might think that `result` points to a function. Actually `result` points to the value returned by the immediate function, in this case the number 4.

Yet another syntax that accomplishes the same results is:

```
var result = (function () {
    return 2 + 2;
})();
```

The previous examples returned a primitive integer value as the result of executing the immediate function. But instead of a primitive value, an immediate function can return any type of value, including another function. You can then use the scope of the immediate function to privately store some data, specific to the inner function you return.

In the next example, the value returned by the immediate function is a function, which will be assigned to the variable `getResult` and will simply return the value of `res`, a value that was precomputed and stored in the immediate function's closure:

```
var getResult = (function () {
    var res = 2 + 2;
```

```
        return function () {
            return res;
        };
    }());
```

Immediate functions can also be used when you define object properties. Imagine you need to define a property that will likely never change during the life of the object, but before you define it a bit of work needs to be performed to figure out the right value. You can use an immediate function to wrap that work and the returned value of the immediate function will become the value of the property. The following code shows an example:

```
var o = {
    message: (function () {
        var who = "me",
            what = "call";
        return what + " " + who;
    }()),
    getMsg: function () {
        return this.message;
    }
};
// usage
o.getMsg(); // "call me"
o.message;  // "call me"
```

In this example, o.message is a string property, not a function, but it needs a function, which executes while the script is loading and which helps define the property.

Benefits and Usage

The immediate function pattern is widely used. It helps you wrap an amount of work you want to do without leaving any global variables behind. All the variables you define will be local to the self-invoking functions and you don't have to worry about polluting the global space with temporary variables.

 Other names for the immediate function pattern include "self-invoking" or "self-executing" function, because the function executes itself as soon as it's defined.

This pattern is also often used in bookmarklets, because bookmarklets run on any page and keeping the global namespace clean (and your bookmarklet code unobtrusive) is critical.

The pattern also enables you to wrap individual features into self-contained modules. Imagine your page is static and works fine without any JavaScript. Then, in the spirit of progressive enhancement, you add a piece of code that enhances the page somehow. You can wrap this code (you can also call it a "module" or a "feature") into an immediate function and make sure the page works fine with and without it. Then you can add more enhancements, remove them, split-test them, allow the user to disable them, and so on.

You can use the following template to define a piece of functionality; let's call it module1:

```
// module1 defined in module1.js
(function () {

    // all the module 1 code ...

}());
```

Following the same template, you can code your other modules. Then when it's time for releasing the code to the live site, you decide which features are ready for prime time and merge the corresponding files using your build script.

Immediate Object Initialization

Another way to protect from global scope pollution, similar to the immediate functions pattern previously described, is the following *immediate object initialization* pattern. This pattern uses an object with an `init()` method, which is executed immediately after the object is created. The `init()` function takes care of all initialization tasks.

Here's an example of the immediate object pattern:

```
({
    // here you can define setting values
    // a.k.a. configuration constants
    max_width: 600,
    max_height: 400,

    // you can also define utility methods
    gimmeMax: function () {
        return this.max_width + "x" + this.max_height;
    },

    // initialize
    init: function () {
        console.log(this.gimmeMax());
        // more init tasks...
    }
}).init();
```

In terms of syntax, you approach this pattern as if you're creating a normal object using the object literal. You also wrap the literal in parentheses (grouping operator), which instructs the JavaScript engine to treat the curly braces as an object literal, not as a code block. (It's not an `if` or a `for` loop.) After you close the parentheses, you invoke the `init()` method immediately.

You can also wrap the object and the `init()` invocation into grouping parentheses instead of wrapping the object only. In other words, both of these work:

```
({...}).init();
({...}.init());
```

The benefits of this pattern are the same as the immediate function pattern: you protect the global namespace while performing the one-off initialization tasks. It may look a little more involved in terms of syntax compared to just wrapping a bunch of code in an anonymous function, but if your initialization tasks are more complicated (as they often are) it adds structure to the whole initialization procedure. For example, private helper functions are clearly distinguishable because they are properties of the temporary object, whereas in an immediate function pattern, they are likely to be just functions scattered around.

A drawback of this pattern is that most JavaScript minifiers may not minify this pattern as efficiently as the code simply wrapped into a function. The private properties and methods will not be renamed to shorter names because, from a minifier's point of view, it's not trivial to do so safely. At the moment of writing, Google's Closure Compiler in "advanced" mode is the only minifier that renames the immediate object's properties to shorter names, turning the preceding example into something like:

```
({d:600,c:400,a:function(){return this.d+"x"+this.c},b:function(){console.log(this.
a())}}).b();
```

 This pattern is mainly suitable for one-off tasks, and there's no access to the object after the `init()` has completed. If you want to keep a reference to the object after it is done, you can easily achieve this by adding `return this;` at the end of `init()`.

Init-Time Branching

Init-time branching (also called load-time branching) is an optimization pattern. When you know that a certain condition will not change throughout the life of the program, it makes sense to test the condition only once. Browser sniffing (or feature detection) is a typical example.

For example, after you've sniffed that `XMLHttpRequest` is supported as a native object, there's no chance that the underlying browser will change in the middle of your program execution and all of a sudden you'll need to deal with ActiveX objects. Because the environment doesn't change, there's no reason for your code to keep sniffing (and reaching the same conclusion) every time you need another XHR object.

Figuring out the computed styles of a DOM element or attaching event handlers are other candidates that can benefit from the init-time branching pattern. Most developers have coded—at least once in their client-side programming life—a utility with methods for attaching and removing event listeners, like in the following example:

```
// BEFORE
var utils = {
    addListener: function (el, type, fn) {
        if (window.addEventListener) {
            el.addEventListener(type, fn, false);
        } else if (document.attachEvent) { // IE
            el.attachEvent('on' + type, fn);
        } else { // older browsers
            el['on' + type] = fn;
        }
    },
    removeListener: function (el, type, fn) {
        // pretty much the same...
    }
};
```

The problem with this code is that it's a bit inefficient. Every time you call `utils.addListener()` or `utils.removeListener()`, the same checks get executed over and over again.

Using init-time branching, you sniff the browser features once, during the initial loading of the script. At that time you redefine how the function will work throughout the lifespan of the page. The following is an example of how you can approach this task:

```
// AFTER

// the interface
var utils = {
    addListener: null,
    removeListener: null
};

// the implementation
if (window.addEventListener) {
    utils.addListener = function (el, type, fn) {
        el.addEventListener(type, fn, false);
    };
    utils.removeListener = function (el, type, fn) {
        el.removeEventListener(type, fn, false);
    };
} else if (document.attachEvent) { // IE
    utils.addListener = function (el, type, fn) {
        el.attachEvent('on' + type, fn);
    };
    utils.removeListener = function (el, type, fn) {
        el.detachEvent('on' + type, fn);
    };
} else { // older browsers
    utils.addListener = function (el, type, fn) {
        el['on' + type] = fn;
    };
    utils.removeListener = function (el, type, fn) {
        el['on' + type] = null;
    };
}
```

Here is the moment to mention a word of caution against browser sniffing. When you use this pattern, don't over-assume browser features. For example, if you've sniffed that the browser doesn't support `window.addEventListener`, don't just assume the browser you're dealing with is IE and it doesn't support `XMLHttpRequest` natively either, although it was true at some point in the browser's history. There might be cases in which you can safely assume that features go together, such as `.addEventListener` and `.removeEventListener`, but in general browser features change independently. The best strategy is to sniff features separately and then use load-time branching to do the sniffing only once.

Function Properties—A Memoization Pattern

Functions are objects, so they can have properties. In fact, they do have properties and methods out-of-the-box. For example, every function, no matter what syntax you use to create it, automatically gets a `length` property containing the number of arguments the function expects:

```
function func(a, b, c) {}
console.log(func.length); // 3
```

You can add custom properties to your functions at any time. One use case for custom properties is to cache the results (the return value) of a function, so the next time the function is called, it doesn't have to redo potentially heavy computations. Caching the results of a function is also known as memoization.

In the following example, the function `myFunc` creates a property `cache`, accessible as usual via `myFunc.cache`. The `cache` property is an object (a hash) where the parameter `param` passed to the function is used as a key and the result of the computation is the value. The result can be any complicated data structure you might need:

```
var myFunc = function (param) {
    if (!myFunc.cache[param]) {
        var result = {};
        // ... expensive operation ...
        myFunc.cache[param] = result;
    }
    return myFunc.cache[param];
};

// cache storage
myFunc.cache = {};
```

The preceding code assumes that the function takes only one argument `param` and it's a primitive data type (such as a string). If you have more parameters and more complex ones, a generic solution would be to serialize them. For example, you can serialize the arguments object as a JSON string and use that string as a key in your `cache` object:

```
var myFunc = function () {

    var cachekey = JSON.stringify(Array.prototype.slice.call(arguments)),
```

```
        result;

    if (!myFunc.cache[cachekey]) {
        result = {};
        // ... expensive operation ...
        myFunc.cache[cachekey] = result;
    }
    return myFunc.cache[cachekey];
};

// cache storage
myFunc.cache = {};
```

Be aware that in serialization, the "identify" of the objects is lost. If you have two different objects that happen to have the same properties, both will share the same cache entry.

Another way to write the previous function is to use `arguments.callee` to refer to the function instead of hardcoding the function name. Although this is currently possible, be aware that `arguments.callee` is not allowed in ECMAScript 5 strict mode:

```
var myFunc = function (param) {

    var f = arguments.callee,
        result;

    if (!f.cache[param]) {
        result = {};
        // ... expensive operation ...
        f.cache[param] = result;
    }
    return f.cache[param];
};

// cache storage
myFunc.cache = {};
```

Configuration Objects

The configuration object pattern is a way to provide cleaner APIs, especially if you're building a library or any other code that will be consumed by other programs.

It's a fact of life that software requirements change as the software is developed and maintained. It often happens that you start working with some requirements in mind, but more functionality gets added afterward.

Imagine you're writing a function called `addPerson()`, which accepts a first and last name and adds a person to a list:

```
function addPerson(first, last) {...}
```

Later you learn that actually the date of birth needs to be stored, too, and optionally the gender and the address. So you modify the function adding the new parameters (carefully putting the optional parameters at the end of the list):

```
function addPerson(first, last, dob, gender, address) {...}
```

At this point the signature of this function is already getting a little longer. And then you learn you need to add a username and it's absolutely required, not optional. Now the caller of the function will have to pass even the optional parameters and be careful not to mix the order of the parameters:

```
addPerson("Bruce", "Wayne", new Date(), null, null, "batman");
```

Passing a large number of parameters is not convenient. A better approach is to substitute all the parameters with only one and make it an object; let's call it conf, for "configuration":

```
addPerson(conf);
```

Then the user of the function can do:

```
var conf = {
    username: "batman",
    first: "Bruce",
    last: "Wayne"
};
addPerson(conf);
```

The pros of the configuration objects are:

- No need to remember the parameters and their order
- You can safely skip optional parameters
- Easier to read and maintain
- Easier to add and remove parameters

The cons of the configuration objects are:

- You need to remember the names of the parameters
- Property names cannot always be safely minified, especially by simpler minifiers

This pattern could be useful when your function creates DOM elements, for example, or in setting the CSS styles of an element, because elements and styles can have a great number of mostly optional attributes and properties.

Curry

The rest of the chapter discusses the topic of currying and *partial* function application. But before we dive into this topic, let's first see what exactly *function application* means.

Function Application

In some purely functional programming languages, a function is not described as being *called* or *invoked*, but rather it's *applied*. In JavaScript we have the same thing—we can apply a function using the method `Function.prototype.apply()`, because functions in JavaScript are actually objects and they have methods.

Here's an example of a function application:

```
// define a function
var sayHi = function (who) {
    return "Hello" + (who ? ", " + who : "") + "!";
};

// invoke a function
sayHi(); // "Hello"
sayHi('world'); // "Hello, world!"

// apply a function
sayHi.apply(null, ["hello"]); // "Hello, hello!"
```

As you can see in the example, both *invoking* a function and *applying* it have the same result. `apply()` takes two parameters: the first one is an object to bind to `this` inside of the function, the second is an array or arguments, which then becomes the array-like `arguments` object available inside the function. If the first parameter is `null`, then `this` points to the global object, which is exactly what happens when you call a function that is not a method of a specific object.

When a function is a method of an object, there's no `null` reference passed around (as in the previous example). Here the object becomes the first argument to `apply()`:

```
var alien = {
    sayHi: function (who) {
        return "Hello" + (who ? ", " + who : "") + "!";
    }
};

alien.sayHi('world'); // "Hello, world!"
alien.sayHi.apply(alien, ["humans"]); // "Hello, humans!"
```

In the preceding snippet, `this` inside of `sayHi()` points to `alien`. In the previous example `this` points to the global object.

As the two examples demonstrate, it turns out that what we think of calling a function is not much more than syntactic sugar, equivalent to a function application.

Note that in addition to `apply()`, there's a `call()` method of the `Function.prototype` object, but it's still just syntax sugar on top of `apply()`. Sometimes it's better to use the sugar: When you have a function that takes only one parameter, you can save the work of creating arrays with just one element:

```
// the second is more efficient, saves an array
alien.sayHi.apply(alien, ["humans"]); // "Hello, humans!"
alien.sayHi.call(alien, "humans"); // "Hello, humans!"
```

Partial Application

Now that we know that calling a function is actually applying a set of arguments to a function, is it possible to pass just a few of the arguments, not all of them? This is actually similar to how you would normally do it, if you were dealing with a math function manually.

Say you have a function `add()` that adds two numbers together: x and y. The following snippet shows how you can approach a solution given that x is 5 and y is 4:

```
// for illustration purposes
// not valid JavaScript

// we have this function
function add(x, y) {
    return x + y;
}

// and we know the arguments
add(5, 4);

// step 1 -- substitute one argument
function add(5, y) {
    return 5 + y;
}

// step 2 -- substitute the other argument
function add(5, 4) {
    return 5 + 4;
}
```

In this snippet the steps 1 and 2 are not valid JavaScript, but this is how you would solve that problem by hand. You take the value of the first argument and substitute the unknown x with the known value 5 throughout the function. Then repeat with the same until you run out of arguments.

Step 1 in this example could be called partial application: we only applied the first argument. When you perform a partial application you don't get a result (a solution), but you get another function instead.

The next snippet demonstrates the use of an imaginary `partialApply()` method:

```
var add = function (x, y) {
    return x + y;
```

```
};

// full application
add.apply(null, [5, 4]); // 9

// partial application
var newadd = add.partialApply(null, [5]);
// applying an argument to the new function
newadd.apply(null, [4]); // 9
```

As you can see, the partial application gives us another function, which can then be called with the other arguments. This would actually be equivalent to something like `add(5)(4)`, because `add(5)` returns a function that can then be called with `(4)`. Again, the familiar `add(5, 4)` may be thought of as not much more than syntactic sugar instead of using `add(5)(4)`.

Now, back to Earth: there's no `partialApply()` method and functions in JavaScript don't behave like this by default. But you can make them, because JavaScript is dynamic enough to allow this.

The process of making a function understand and handle partial application is called currying.

Currying

Currying has nothing to do with the spicy Indian dish; it comes from the name of the mathematician Haskell Curry. (The Haskell programming language is also named after him.) Currying is a transformation process—we transform a function. An alternative name for currying could be *schönfinkelisation*, after the name of another mathematician, Moses Schönfinkel, the original inventor of this transformation.

So how do we *schönfinkelify* (or *schönfinkelize* or *curry*) a function? Other functional languages may have that built right into the language itself and all functions are curried by default. In JavaScript we can modify the `add()` function into a curried one that will handle partial application.

Let's take an example:

```
// a curried add()
// accepts partial list of arguments
function add(x, y) {
    var oldx = x, oldy = y;
    if (typeof oldy === "undefined") { // partial
        return function (newy) {
            return oldx + newy;
        };
    }
    // full application
    return x + y;
}

// test
```

```
typeof add(5); // "function"
add(3)(4); // 7

// create and store a new function
var add2000 = add(2000);
add2000(10); // 2010
```

In this snippet, the first time you call add(), it creates a closure around the inner function it returns. The closure stores the original values x and y into private variables oldx and oldy. The first one, oldx, is used when the inner function executes. If there's no partial application and both x and y are passed, the function proceeds to simply add them. This implementation of add() is a little more verbose than needed, just for illustration purposes. A more compact version is shown in the next snippet, where there's no oldx and oldy, simply because the original x is stored in the closure implicitly and we reuse y as a local variable instead of creating a new variable newy as we did in the previous example:

```
// a curried add
// accepts partial list of arguments
function add(x, y) {
    if (typeof y === "undefined") { // partial
        return function (y) {
            return x + y;
        };
    }
    // full application
    return x + y;
}
```

In these examples, the function add() itself took care of partial applications. But can we do the same in a more generic fashion? In other words, can we transform any function into a new one that accepts partial parameters? The next snippet shows an example of a general-purpose function, let's call it schonfinkelize(), which does just that. We use the name schonfinkelize() partially because it's a challenge to pronounce and partially because it sounds like a verb (using "curry" could be ambiguous) and we need a verb to denote that this is a transformation of a function.

Here is the general-purpose currying function:

```
function schonfinkelize(fn) {
    var slice = Array.prototype.slice,
        stored_args = slice.call(arguments, 1);
    return function () {
        var new_args = slice.call(arguments),
            args = stored_args.concat(new_args);
        return fn.apply(null, args);
    };
}
```

The schonfinkelize() function is probably a little more complicated than it should be, but only because arguments is not a real array in JavaScript. Borrowing the slice() method from Array.prototype helps us turn arguments into an array and work more conveniently with it. When `schonfinkelize()` is called the first time, it stores a private reference to the `slice()` method (called `slice`) and also stores the arguments it was called with (into `stored_args`), only stripping the first, because the first argument is the function being curried. Then `schonfinkelize()` returns a new function. When the new function is called, it has access (via the closure) to the already privately stored arguments `stored_args` and the `slice` reference. The new function has to merge only the old partially applied arguments (`stored_args`) with the new ones (`new_args`) and then apply them to the original function `fn` (also privately available in the closure).

Now armed with a general-purpose way of making any function curried, let's give it a try with a few tests:

```
// a normal function
function add(x, y) {
    return x + y;
}

// curry a function to get a new function
var newadd = schonfinkelize(add, 5);
newadd(4); // 9

// another option -- call the new function directly
schonfinkelize(add, 6)(7); // 13
```

The transformation function `schonfinkelize()` is not limited to single parameters or to single-step currying. Here are some more usage examples:

```
// a normal function
function add(a, b, c, d, e) {
    return a + b + c + d + e;
}

// works with any number of arguments
schonfinkelize(add, 1, 2, 3)(5, 5); // 16

// two-step currying
var addOne = schonfinkelize(add, 1);
addOne(10, 10, 10, 10); // 41
var addSix = schonfinkelize(addOne, 2, 3);
addSix(5, 5); // 16
```

When to Use Currying

When you find yourself calling the same function and passing mostly the same parameters, then the function is probably a good candidate for currying. You can create a new function dynamically by partially applying a set of arguments to your function. The new function will keep the repeated parameters stored (so you don't have to pass them every time) and will use them to pre-fill the full list of arguments that the original function expects.

Summary

In JavaScript the knowledge and proper use of functions is critical. This chapter discussed the background and terminology related to functions. You learned about the two important features of functions in JavaScript, namely:

1. Functions are *first-class objects*; they can be passed around as values and augmented with properties and methods.
2. Functions provide local *scope*, which other curly braces do not. Also something to keep in mind is that declarations of local variables get hoisted to the top of the local scope.

The syntax for creating functions includes:

1. *Named function expressions*
2. *Function expressions* (the same as the above, but missing a name), also known as *anonymous functions*
3. *Function declarations*, similar to the function syntax in other languages

After covering the background and syntax of functions, you learned about a number of useful patterns, which can be grouped into the following categories:

1. *API patterns*, which help you provide better and cleaner interfaces to your functions. These patterns include:

   Callback patterns
   Pass a function as an argument

   Configuration objects
   Help keep the number of arguments to a function under control

   Returning functions
   When the return value of one function is another function

   Currying
   When new functions are created based on existing ones plus a partial list of arguments

2. *Initialization patterns*, which help you perform initialization and setup tasks (very common when it comes to web pages and applications) in a clearer, structured way without polluting the global namespace with temporary variables. These include:

   Immediate functions
   Executed as soon as they are defined

   Immediate object initialization
   Initialization tasks structured in an anonymous object that provides a method to be called immediately

Init-time branching
> Helps branch code only once during initial code execution, as opposed to many times later during the life of the application

3. *Performance patterns*, which help speed up the code. These include:

Memoization
> Using function properties so that computed values are not computed again

Self-defining functions
> Overwrite themselves with new bodies to do less work from the second invocation and after

CHAPTER 5

Object Creation Patterns

Creating objects in JavaScript is easy—you either use the object literal or you use constructor functions. In this chapter we go beyond that and see some additional patterns for object creation.

The JavaScript language is simple and straightforward and often there's no special syntax for features you may be used to in other languages, such as namespaces, modules, packages, private properties, and static members. This chapter takes you through common patterns to implement, substitute, or just think differently about those features.

We take a look at namespacing, dependency declaration, module pattern, and sandbox patterns—they help you organize and structure your application code and mitigate the effect of the implied globals. Other topics of discussion include private and privileged members, static and private static members, object constants, chaining, and one class-inspired way to define constructors.

Namespace Pattern

Namespaces help reduce the number of globals required by our programs and at the same time also help avoid naming collisions or excessive name prefixing.

JavaScript doesn't have namespaces built into the language syntax, but this is a feature that is quite easy to achieve. Instead of polluting the global scope with a lot of functions, objects, and other variables, you can create one (and ideally only one) global object for your application or library. Then you can add all the functionality to that object.

Consider the following example:

```
// BEFORE: 5 globals
// Warning: antipattern

// constructors
function Parent() {}
function Child() {}

// a variable
```

```
var some_var = 1;

// some objects
var module1 = {};
module1.data = {a: 1, b: 2};
var module2 = {};
```

You can refactor this type of code by creating a single global object for your application, called, for example, MYAPP, and change all your functions and variables to become properties of your global object:

```
// AFTER: 1 global

// global object
var MYAPP = {};

// constructors
MYAPP.Parent = function () {};
MYAPP.Child = function () {};

// a variable
MYAPP.some_var = 1;

// an object container
MYAPP.modules = {};

// nested objects
MYAPP.modules.module1 = {};
MYAPP.modules.module1.data = {a: 1, b: 2};
MYAPP.modules.module2 = {};
```

For the name of the global namespace object, you can pick, for example, the name of your application or library, your domain name, or your company name. Often developers use the convention of making the global variable ALL CAPS, so it stands out to the readers of the code. (But keep in mind that all caps are also often used for constants.)

This pattern is a good way to namespace your code and to avoid naming collisions in your own code, and collisions between your code and third-party code on the same page, such as JavaScript libraries or widgets. This pattern is highly recommended and perfectly applicable for many tasks, but it does have some drawbacks:

- A bit more to type; prefixing every variable and function does add up in the total amount of code that needs to be downloaded
- Only one global instance means that any part of the code can modify the global instance and the rest of the functionality gets the updated state
- Long nested names mean longer (slower) property resolution lookups

The sandbox pattern discussed later in the chapter addresses these drawbacks.

General Purpose Namespace Function

As the complexity of a program grows and some parts of code get split into different files and included conditionally, it becomes unsafe to just assume that your code is the first to define a certain namespace or a property inside of it. Some of the properties you're adding to the namespace may already exist, and you could be overwriting them. Therefore before adding a property or creating a namespace, it's best to check first that it doesn't already exist, as shown in this example:

```
// unsafe
var MYAPP = {};
// better
if (typeof MYAPP === "undefined") {
    var MYAPP = {};
}
// or shorter
var MYAPP = MYAPP || {};
```

You can see how these added checks can quickly result in a lot of repeating code. For example, if you want to define MYAPP.modules.module2, you'll have to make three checks, one for each object or property you're defining. That's why it's handy to have a reusable function that takes care of the namespacing details. Let's call this function namespace() and use it like so:

```
// using a namespace function
MYAPP.namespace('MYAPP.modules.module2');

// equivalent to:
// var MYAPP = {
//     modules: {
//         module2: {}
//     }
// };
```

Next is an example implementation of the namespacing function. This implementation is nondestructive, meaning that if a namespace exists, it won't be re-created:

```
var MYAPP = MYAPP || {};

MYAPP.namespace = function (ns_string) {
    var parts = ns_string.split('.'),
        parent = MYAPP,
        i;

    // strip redundant leading global
    if (parts[0] === "MYAPP") {
        parts = parts.slice(1);
    }

    for (i = 0; i < parts.length; i += 1) {
        // create a property if it doesn't exist
        if (typeof parent[parts[i]] === "undefined") {
            parent[parts[i]] = {};
        }
```

```
        parent = parent[parts[i]];
    }
    return parent;
};
```

This implementation enables all of these uses:

```
// assign returned value to a local var
var module2 = MYAPP.namespace('MYAPP.modules.module2');
module2 === MYAPP.modules.module2; // true

// skip initial `MYAPP`
MYAPP.namespace('modules.module51');

// long namespace
MYAPP.namespace('once.upon.a.time.there.was.this.long.nested.property');
```

Figure 5-1 shows how the namespaces in the preceding example look like when inspected in Firebug.

```
┃┃    window  >   Object
    ▼ modules                                   Object { module2=Object,  more... }
        module2                                 Object { }
        module51                                Object { }
    ▼ once                                       Object { upon=Object }
      ▼ upon                                      Object { a=Object }
        ▼ a                                        Object { time=Object }
          ▼ time                                    Object { there=Object }
            ▼ there                                  Object { was=Object }
              ▼ was                                   Object { this=Object }
                ▼ this                                 Object { long=Object }
                  ▼ long                                Object { nested=Object }
                    ▼ nested                             Object { property=Object }
                        property                          Object { }
        namespace                               function()
```

Figure 5-1. MYAPP namespace inspected in Firebug

Declaring Dependencies

JavaScript libraries are often modular and namespaced, which enables you to include only the modules you require. For example, in YUI2 there's a global variable YAHOO, which serves as a namespace, and then modules that are properties of the global variable, such as YAHOO.util.Dom (the DOM module) and YAHOO.util.Event (Events module).

It's a good idea to declare the modules your code relies on at the top of your function or module. The declaration involves creating only a local variable and pointing to the desired module:

```
var myFunction = function () {
    // dependencies
    var event = YAHOO.util.Event,
        dom = YAHOO.util.Dom;

    // use event and dom variables
    // for the rest of the function...
};
```

This is an extremely simple pattern, but at the same time it has numerous benefits:

- Explicit declaration of dependencies signals to the users of your code the specific script files that they need to make sure are included in the page.

- Upfront declaration at the top of the function makes it easy to find and resolve dependencies.

- Working with a local variable (such as dom) is always faster than working with a global (such as YAHOO) and even faster than working with nested properties of a global variable (such as YAHOO.util.Dom), resulting in better performance. When following this dependency declaration pattern, the global symbol resolution is performed only once in the function. After that the local variable is used, which is much faster.

- Smaller code after minification—most minification tools will rename local variables (so event will likely become just one character such as A) but willl not rename global variables, because it's usually not safe to do so. (Google Closure compiler in "advanced" mode is an exception, but even then you have to be careful.)

The following snippet is an illustration of the effect of the dependency declaration pattern on the minified code. Although test2(), which follows the pattern, looks a bit more involved because it requires more lines of code and an extra variable, it actually results in less code after minification, meaning less code the user has to download:

```
function test1() {
    alert(MYAPP.modules.m1);
    alert(MYAPP.modules.m2);
    alert(MYAPP.modules.m51);
}

/*
minified test1 body:
alert(MYAPP.modules.m1);alert(MYAPP.modules.m2);alert(MYAPP.modules.m51)
*/

function test2() {
    var modules = MYAPP.modules;
    alert(modules.m1);
    alert(modules.m2);
    alert(modules.m51);
}

/*
minified test2 body:
```

```
    var a=MYAPP.modules;alert(a.m1);alert(a.m2);alert(a.m51)
    */
```

Private Properties and Methods

JavaScript has no special syntax to denote private, protected, or public properties and methods, unlike Java or other languages. All object members are public:

```
var myobj = {
    myprop: 1,
    getProp: function () {
        return this.myprop;
    }
};
console.log(myobj.myprop); // `myprop` is publicly accessible
console.log(myobj.getProp()); // getProp() is public too
```

The same is true when you use constructor functions to create objects; all members are still public:

```
function Gadget() {
    this.name = 'iPod';
    this.stretch = function () {
        return 'iPad';
    };
}
var toy = new Gadget();
console.log(toy.name); // `name` is public
console.log(toy.stretch()); // stretch() is public
```

Private Members

Although the language doesn't have special syntax for private members, you can implement them using a closure. Your constructor functions create a closure and any variables that are part of the closure scope are not exposed outside the constructor. However, these private variables are available to the public methods: methods defined inside the constructor and exposed as part of the returned objects. Let's see an example where name is a private member, not accessible outside the constructor:

```
function Gadget() {
    // private member
    var name = 'iPod';
    // public function
    this.getName = function () {
        return name;
    };
}
var toy = new Gadget();

// `name` is undefined, it's private
console.log(toy.name); // undefined
```

```
// public method has access to `name`
console.log(toy.getName()); // "iPod"
```

As you can see, it's easy to achieve privacy in JavaScript. All you need to do is wrap the data you want to keep private in a function and make sure it's local to the function, which means not making it available outside the function.

Privileged Methods

The notion of *privileged methods* doesn't involve any specific syntax; it's just a name given to the public methods that have access to the private members (and hence have more privileges).

In the previous example, getName() is a privileged method because it has "special" access to the private property name.

Privacy Failures

There are some edge cases when you're concerned about privacy:

- Some earlier versions of Firefox enable a second parameter to be passed to eval() that is a context object enabling you to sneak into the private scope of the function. Similarly the __parent__ property in Mozilla Rhino would enable you access to private scope. These edge cases don't apply to widely used browsers today.

- When you're directly returning a private variable from a privileged method and this variable happens to be an object or array, then outside code can modify the private variable because it's passed by reference.

Let's examine the second case a little more closely. The following implementation of Gadget looks innocent:

```
function Gadget() {
    // private member
    var specs = {
        screen_width:  320,
        screen_height: 480,
        color: "white"
    };

    // public function
    this.getSpecs = function () {
        return specs;
    };
}
```

The problem here is that getSpecs() returns a reference to the specs object. This enables the user of Gadget to modify the seemingly hidden and private specs:

```
var toy = new Gadget(),
    specs = toy.getSpecs();
```

```
specs.color = "black";
specs.price = "free";

console.dir(toy.getSpecs());
```

This result of printing to the Firebug console is shown in Figure 5-2.

color	"black"
price	"free"
screen_height	480
screen_width	320

Figure 5-2. The private object was modified

The solution to this unexpected behavior is to be careful not to pass references to objects and arrays you want to keep private. One way to achieve this is to have `getSpecs()` return a new object containing only some of the data that could be interesting to the consumer of the object. This is also known as Principle of Least Authority (POLA), which states that you should never give more than needed. In this case, if the consumer of Gadget is interested whether the gadget fits a certain box, it needs only the dimensions. So instead of giving out everything, you can create `getDimensions()`, which returns a new object containing only width and height. You may not need to implement `getSpecs()` at all.

Another approach, when you need to pass all the data, is to create a copy of the `specs` object, using a general-purpose object-cloning function. The next chapter offers two such functions—one is called `extend()` and does a shallow copy of the given object (copies only the top-level parameters). The other one is called `extendDeep()`, which does a deep copy, recursively copying all properties and their nested properties.

Object Literals and Privacy

So far we've looked only at examples of using constructors to achieve privacy. But what about the cases when your objects are created with object literals? Is it still possible to have private members?

As you saw before, all you need is a function to wrap the private data. So in the case of object literals, you can use the closure created by an additional anonymous immediate function. Here's an example:

```
var myobj; // this will be the object
(function () {
    // private members
    var name = "my, oh my";

    // implement the public part
    // note -- no `var`
```

```
    myobj = {
        // privileged method
        getName: function () {
            return name;
        }
    };
}());

myobj.getName(); // "my, oh my"
```

The same idea but with slightly different implementation is given in the following example:

```
var myobj = (function () {
    // private members
    var name = "my, oh my";

    // implement the public part
    return {
        getName: function () {
            return name;
        }
    };
}());

myobj.getName(); // "my, oh my"
```

This example is also the bare bones of what is known as "module pattern," which we examine in just a bit.

Prototypes and Privacy

One drawback of the private members when used with constructors is that they are re-created every time the constructor is invoked to create a new object.

This is actually a problem with any members you add to this inside of constructors. To avoid the duplication of effort and save memory, you can add common properties and methods to the prototype property of the constructor. This way the common parts are shared among all the instances created with the same constructor. You can also share the hidden private members among the instances. To do so you can use a combination of two patterns: private properties inside constructors and private properties in object literals. Because the prototype property is just an object, it can be created with the object literals.

Here's an example of how you can achieve this:

```
function Gadget() {
    // private member
    var name = 'iPod';
    // public function
    this.getName = function () {
        return name;
    };
```

```
    }

    Gadget.prototype = (function () {
        // private member
        var browser = "Mobile Webkit";
        // public prototype members
        return {
            getBrowser: function () {
                return browser;
            }
        };
    }());

    var toy = new Gadget();
    console.log(toy.getName()); // privileged "own" method
    console.log(toy.getBrowser()); // privileged prototype method
```

Revealing Private Functions As Public Methods

The revelation pattern is about having private methods, which you also expose as public methods. This could be useful when all the functionality in an object is critical for the workings of the object and you want to protect it as much as possible. But at the same time you want to provide public access to some of this functionality because that could be useful, too. When you expose methods publicly, you make them vulnerable; some of the users of your public API may modify it, even involuntarily. In ECMAScript 5 you have the option to freeze an object, but not in the previous versions of the language. Enter the revelation pattern (the term coined by Christian Heilmann originally was "revealing module pattern").

Let's take an example, building on top of one of the privacy patterns—the private members in object literals:

```
var myarray;

(function () {

    var astr = "[object Array]",
        toString = Object.prototype.toString;

    function isArray(a) {
        return toString.call(a) === astr;
    }

    function indexOf(haystack, needle) {
        var i = 0,
            max = haystack.length;
        for (; i < max; i += 1) {
            if (haystack[i] === needle) {
                return i;
            }
        }
        return -1;
    }
```

```
    myarray = {
        isArray: isArray,
        indexOf: indexOf,
        inArray: indexOf
    };

}());
```

Here you have two private variables and two private functions—isArray() and indexOf(). Toward the end of the immediate function, the object myarray is populated with the functionality you decide is appropriate to make publicly available. In this case the same private indexOf() is exposed as both ECMAScript 5–style indexOf and PHP-inspired inArray. Testing the new myarray object:

```
myarray.isArray([1,2]); // true
myarray.isArray({0: 1}); // false
myarray.indexOf(["a", "b", "z"], "z"); // 2
myarray.inArray(["a", "b", "z"], "z"); // 2
```

Now if something unexpected happens, for example, to the public indexOf(), the private indexOf() is still safe and therefore inArray() will continue to work:

```
myarray.indexOf = null;
myarray.inArray(["a", "b", "z"], "z"); // 2
```

Module Pattern

The module pattern is widely used because it provides structure and helps organize your code as it grows. Unlike other languages, JavaScript doesn't have special syntax for packages, but the module pattern provides the tools to create self-contained decoupled pieces of code, which can be treated as black boxes of functionality and added, replaced, or removed according to the (ever-changing) requirements of the software you're writing.

The module pattern is a combination of several patterns described so far in the book, namely:

- Namespaces
- Immediate functions
- Private and privileged members
- Declaring dependencies

The first step is setting up a namespace. Let's use the namespace() function from earlier in this chapter and start an example utility module that provides useful array methods:

```
MYAPP.namespace('MYAPP.utilities.array');
```

The next step is defining the module. The pattern uses an immediate function that will provide private scope if privacy is needed. The immediate function returns an object—

the actual module with its public interface, which will be available to the consumers of the module:

```
MYAPP.utilities.array = (function () {
    return {
        // todo...
    };
}());
```

Next, let's add some methods to the public interface:

```
MYAPP.utilities.array = (function () {
    return {
        inArray: function (needle, haystack) {
            // ...
        },
        isArray: function (a) {
            // ...
        }
    };
}());
```

Using the private scope provided by the immediate function, you can declare some private properties and methods as needed. Right at the top of the immediate function will also be the place to declare any dependencies your module might have. Following the variable declarations, you can optionally place any one-off initialization code that helps set up the module. The final result is an object returned by the immediate function that contains the public API of your module:

```
MYAPP.namespace('MYAPP.utilities.array');

MYAPP.utilities.array = (function () {

        // dependencies
    var uobj  = MYAPP.utilities.object,
        ulang = MYAPP.utilities.lang,

        // private properties
        array_string = "[object Array]",
        ops = Object.prototype.toString;

        // private methods
        // ...

        // end var

    // optionally one-time init procedures
    // ...

    // public API
    return {

        inArray: function (needle, haystack) {
            for (var i = 0, max = haystack.length; i < max; i += 1) {
                if (haystack[i] === needle) {
```

```
                    return true;
                }
            }
        },

        isArray: function (a) {
            return ops.call(a) === array_string;
        }
        // ... more methods and properties
    };
}());
```

The module pattern is a widely used and highly recommended way to organize your code, especially as it grows.

Revealing Module Pattern

We already discussed the revelation pattern in this chapter while looking at the privacy patterns. The module pattern can be organized in a similar way, where all the methods are kept private and you only expose those that you decide at the end, while setting up the public API.

The above can become:

```
MYAPP.utilities.array = (function () {

        // private properties
    var array_string = "[object Array]",
        ops = Object.prototype.toString,

        // private methods
        inArray = function (haystack, needle) {
            for (var i = 0, max = haystack.length; i < max; i += 1) {
                if (haystack[i] === needle) {
                    return i;
                }
            }
            return -1;
        },
        isArray = function (a) {
            return ops.call(a) === array_string;
        };
        // end var

    // revealing public API
    return {
        isArray: isArray,
        indexOf: inArray
    };
}());
```

Modules That Create Constructors

The preceding example produced an object MYAPP.utilities.array, but sometimes it's more convenient to create your objects using constructor functions. You can still do that using the module pattern. The only difference is that the immediate function that wraps the module will return a function at the end, and not an object.

Consider the following example of the module pattern that creates a constructor function MYAPP.utilities.Array:

```
MYAPP.namespace('MYAPP.utilities.Array');

MYAPP.utilities.Array = (function () {

        // dependencies
    var uobj  = MYAPP.utilities.object,
        ulang = MYAPP.utilities.lang,

        // private properties and methods...
        Constr;

        // end var

    // optionally one-time init procedures
    // ...

    // public API -- constructor
    Constr = function (o) {
        this.elements = this.toArray(o);
    };
    // public API -- prototype
    Constr.prototype = {
        constructor: MYAPP.utilities.Array,
        version: "2.0",
        toArray: function (obj) {
            for (var i = 0, a = [], len = obj.length; i < len; i += 1) {
                a[i] = obj[i];
            }
            return a;
        }
    };

    // return the constructor
    // to be assigned to the new namespace
    return Constr;

}());
```

The way to use this new constructor will be like so:

```
var arr = new MYAPP.utilities.Array(obj);
```

Importing Globals into a Module

In a common variation of the pattern, you can pass arguments to the immediate function that wraps the module. You can pass any values, but usually these are references to global variables and even the global object itself. Importing globals helps speed up the global symbol resolution inside the immediate function, because the imported variables become locals for the function:

```
MYAPP.utilities.module = (function (app, global) {

    // references to the global object
    // and to the global app namespace object
    // are now localized

}(MYAPP, this));
```

Sandbox Pattern

The sandbox pattern addresses the drawbacks of the namespacing pattern, namely:

* Reliance on a single global variable to be the application's global. In the namespacing pattern, there is no way to have two versions of the same application or library run on the same page, because they both need the same global symbol name, for example, `MYAPP`.

* Long, dotted names to type and resolve at runtime, for example, `MYAPP.utilities.array`.

As the name suggests, the sandbox pattern provides an environment for the modules to "play" without affecting other modules and their personal sandboxes.

The pattern is heavily used in YUI version 3, for example, but keep in mind that the following discussion is a sample reference implementation and does not attempt to describe how YUI3's sandbox implementation works.

A Global Constructor

In the namespacing pattern you have one global object; in the sandbox pattern the single global is a constructor: let's call it `Sandbox()`. You create objects using this constructor, and you also pass a callback function, which becomes the isolated sandboxed environment for your code.

Using the sandbox will look like this:

```
new Sandbox(function (box) {
    // your code here...
});
```

The object `box` will be like `MYAPP` in the namespacing example—it will have all the library functionality you need to make your code work.

Let's add two more things to the pattern:

- With some magic (enforcing new pattern from Chapter 3), you can assume new and not require it when creating the object.
- The Sandbox() constructor can accept an additional configuration argument (or arguments) specifying names of modules required for this object instance. We want the code to be modular, so most of the functionality Sandbox() provides will be contained in modules.

With these two additional features, let's see some examples of what the code for instantiating objects will look like.

You can omit new and create an object that uses some fictional "ajax" and "event" modules like so:

```
Sandbox(['ajax', 'event'], function (box) {
    // console.log(box);
});
```

This example is similar to the preceding one, but this time module names are passed as individual arguments:

```
Sandbox('ajax', 'dom', function (box) {
    // console.log(box);
});
```

And how about using a wildcard "*" argument to mean "use all available modules"? For convenience, let's also say that when no modules are passed, the sandbox will assume '*'. So two ways to use all available modules will be like:

```
Sandbox('*', function (box) {
    // console.log(box);
});

Sandbox(function (box) {
    // console.log(box);
});
```

And one more example of using the pattern illustrates how you can instantiate sandbox objects multiple times—and you can even nest them one within the other without the two interfering:

```
Sandbox('dom', 'event', function (box) {

    // work with dom and event

    Sandbox('ajax', function (box) {
        // another sandboxed "box" object
        // this "box" is not the same as
        // the "box" outside this function

        //...

        // done with Ajax
```

```
    });

    // no trace of Ajax module here

});
```

As you can see from these examples, when using the sandbox pattern, you can protect the global namespace by having your code wrapped into callback functions.

If you need, you can also use the fact that functions are objects and store some data as "static" properties of the `Sandbox()` constructor.

And, finally, you can have different instances depending on the type of modules you need and those instances work independently of each other.

Now let's see how you can approach implementing the `Sandbox()` constructor and its modules to support all this functionality.

Adding Modules

Before implementing the actual constructor, let's see how we can approach adding modules.

The `Sandbox()` constructor function is also an object, so you can add a static property called `modules` to it. This property will be another object containing key-value pairs where the keys are the names of the modules and the values are the functions that implement each module:

```
Sandbox.modules = {};

Sandbox.modules.dom = function (box) {
    box.getElement = function () {};
    box.getStyle = function () {};
    box.foo = "bar";
};

Sandbox.modules.event = function (box) {
    // access to the Sandbox prototype if needed:
    // box.constructor.prototype.m = "mmm";
    box.attachEvent = function () {};
    box.detachEvent = function () {};
};

Sandbox.modules.ajax = function (box) {
    box.makeRequest = function () {};
    box.getResponse = function () {};
};
```

In this example we added modules `dom`, `event`, and `ajax`, which are common pieces of functionality in every library or complex web application.

The functions that implement each module accept the current instance `box` as a parameter and may add additional properties and methods to that instance.

Implementing the Constructor

Finally, let's implement the `Sandbox()` constructor (naturally, you would want to re-name this type of constructor to something that makes sense for your library or application):

```
function Sandbox() {
        // turning arguments into an array
    var args = Array.prototype.slice.call(arguments),
        // the last argument is the callback
        callback = args.pop(),
        // modules can be passed as an array or as individual parameters
        modules = (args[0] && typeof args[0] === "string") ? args : args[0],
        i;

    // make sure the function is called
    // as a constructor
    if (!(this instanceof Sandbox)) {
        return new Sandbox(modules, callback);
    }

    // add properties to `this` as needed:
    this.a = 1;
    this.b = 2;

    // now add modules to the core `this` object
    // no modules or "*" both mean "use all modules"
    if (!modules || modules === '*') {
        modules = [];
        for (i in Sandbox.modules) {
            if (Sandbox.modules.hasOwnProperty(i)) {
                modules.push(i);
            }
        }
    }

    // initialize the required modules
    for (i = 0; i < modules.length; i += 1) {
        Sandbox.modules[modules[i]](this);
    }

    // call the callback
    callback(this);
}

// any prototype properties as needed
Sandbox.prototype = {
    name: "My Application",
    version: "1.0",
    getName: function () {
        return this.name;
    }
};
```

The key items in the implementation are:

- There's a check whether this is an instance of Sandbox and if not (meaning Sandbox() was called without new), we call the function again as a constructor.
- You can add properties to this inside the constructor. You can also add properties to the prototype of the constructor.
- The required modules can be passed as an array of module names, or as individual arguments, or with the * wildcard (or omitted), which means we should load all available modules. Notice that in this example implementation we don't worry about loading required functionality from additional files, but that's definitely an option. This is something supported by YUI3 for example. You can load only the most basic module (also known as a "seed") and whatever modules you require will be loaded from external files using a naming convention where the filenames correspond to module names.
- When we know the required modules, we initialize them, which means we call the function that implements each module.
- The last argument to the constructor is the callback. The callback will be invoked at the end using the newly created instance. This callback is actually the user's sandbox, and it gets a box object populated with all the requested functionality.

Static Members

Static properties and methods are those that don't change from one instance to another. In class-based languages, static members are created using special syntax and then used as if they were members of the class itself. For example, a static method max() of some MathUtils class would be invoked like MathUtils.max(3, 5). This is an example of a public static member, which can be used without having to create an instance of the class. There can also be private static members—not visible to the consumer of the class but still shared among all the instances of the class. Let's see how to implement both private and public static members in JavaScript.

Public Static Members

In JavaScript there's no special syntax to denote static members. But you can have the same syntax as in a "classy" language by using a constructor function and adding properties to it. This works because constructors, like all other functions, are objects and they can have properties. The memoization pattern discussed in the previous chapter employed the same idea—adding properties to a function.

The following example defines a constructor Gadget with a static method isShiny() and a regular instance method setPrice(). The method isShiny() is a static method because it doesn't need a specific gadget object to work (just like you don't need a particular gadget to figure out that all gadgets are shiny). setPrice(), on the other hand, needs an object, because gadgets can be priced differently:

```
// constructor
var Gadget = function () {};

// a static method
Gadget.isShiny = function () {
    return "you bet";
};

// a normal method added to the prototype
Gadget.prototype.setPrice = function (price) {
    this.price = price;
};
```

Now let's call these methods. The static isShiny() is invoked directly on the constructor, whereas the regular method needs an instance:

```
// calling a static method
Gadget.isShiny(); // "you bet"

// creating an instance and calling a method
var iphone = new Gadget();
iphone.setPrice(500);
```

Attempting to call an instance method statically won't work; same for calling a static method using the instance iphone object:

```
typeof Gadget.setPrice; // "undefined"
typeof iphone.isShiny;  // "undefined"
```

Sometimes it could be convenient to have the static methods working with an instance too. This is easy to achieve by simply adding a new method to the prototype, which serves as a façade pointing to the original static method:

```
Gadget.prototype.isShiny = Gadget.isShiny;
iphone.isShiny(); // "you bet"
```

In such cases you need to be careful if you use this inside the static method. When you do Gadget.isShiny() then this inside isShiny() will refer to the Gadget constructor function. If you do iphone.isShiny() then this will point to iphone.

One last example shows how you can have the same method being called statically and nonstatically and behave slightly different, depending on the invocation pattern. Here instanceof helps determine how the method was called:

```
// constructor
var Gadget = function (price) {
    this.price = price;
};

// a static method
Gadget.isShiny = function () {

    // this always works
```

```
    var msg = "you bet";

    if (this instanceof Gadget) {
        // this only works if called non-statically
        msg += ", it costs $" + this.price + '!';
    }

    return msg;
};

// a normal method added to the prototype
Gadget.prototype.isShiny = function () {
    return Gadget.isShiny.call(this);
};
```

Testing a static method call:

```
Gadget.isShiny(); // "you bet"
```

Testing an instance, nonstatic call:

```
var a = new Gadget('499.99');
a.isShiny(); // "you bet, it costs $499.99!"
```

Private Static Members

The discussion so far was on public static methods; now let's take a look at how you can implement *private static* members. By private static members, we mean members that are:

- Shared by all the objects created with the same constructor function
- Not accessible outside the constructor

Let's look at an example where counter is a private static property in the constructor Gadget. In this chapter there was already a discussion on private properties, so this part is still the same—you need a function to act as a closure and wrap around the private members. Then let's have the same wrapper function execute immediately and return a new function. The returned function value is assigned to the variable Gadget and becomes the new constructor:

```
var Gadget = (function () {

    // static variable/property
    var counter = 0;

    // returning the new implementation
    // of the constructor
    return function () {
        console.log(counter += 1);
    };

}()); // execute immediately
```

The new `Gadget` constructor simply increments and logs the private `counter`. Testing with several instances you can see that `counter` is indeed shared among all instances:

```
var g1 = new Gadget(); // logs 1
var g2 = new Gadget(); // logs 2
var g3 = new Gadget(); // logs 3
```

Because we're incrementing the `counter` with one for every object, this static property becomes an ID that uniquely identifies each object created with the `Gadget` constructor. The unique identifier could be useful, so why not expose it via a privileged method? Below is an example that builds upon the previous and adds a privileged method `getLastId()` to access the static private property:

```
// constructor
var Gadget = (function () {

    // static variable/property
    var counter = 0,
        NewGadget;

    // this will become the
    // new constructor implementation
    NewGadget = function () {
        counter += 1;
    };

    // a privileged method
    NewGadget.prototype.getLastId = function () {
        return counter;
    };

    // overwrite the constructor
    return NewGadget;

}()); // execute immediately
```

Testing the new implementation:

```
var iphone = new Gadget();
iphone.getLastId(); // 1
var ipod = new Gadget();
ipod.getLastId();   // 2
var ipad = new Gadget();
ipad.getLastId();   // 3
```

Static properties (both private and public) can be quite handy. They can contain methods and data that are not instance-specific and don't get re-created with every instance. In Chapter 7, when we discuss the singleton pattern, you can see an example implementation that uses static properties to implement class-like singleton constructors.

Object Constants

There are no constants in JavaScript, although many modern environments may offer you the const statement to create constants.

As a workaround, a common approach is to use a naming convention and make variables that shouldn't be changed stand out using all caps. This convention is actually used in the built-in JavaScript objects:

```
Math.PI; // 3.141592653589793
Math.SQRT2; // 1.4142135623730951
Number.MAX_VALUE; // 1.7976931348623157e+308
```

For your own constants you can adopt the same naming convention and add them as static properties to the constructor function:

```
// constructor
var Widget = function () {
    // implementation...
};

// constants
Widget.MAX_HEIGHT = 320;
Widget.MAX_WIDTH = 480;
```

The same convention can be applied for objects created with a literal; the constants could be normal properties with uppercase names.

If you really want to have an immutable value, you can create a private property and provide a getter method, but no setter. This is probably overkill in many cases when you can get by with a simple convention, but it is still an option.

The following example is an implementation of a general-purpose constant object, which provides these methods:

set(*name, value*)
> To define a new constant

isDefined(*name*)
> To check whether a constant exists

get(*name*)
> To get the value of a constant

In this implementation, only primitive values are allowed as constants. Also some extra care is taken to assure that it's okay to declare constants with names that happen to be names of built-in properties, such as toString or hasOwnProperty by using a hasOwnProperty() check and additionally prepending all constant names with a randomly generated prefix:

```
var constant = (function () {
    var constants = {},
        ownProp = Object.prototype.hasOwnProperty,
        allowed = {
```

```
                string: 1,
                number: 1,
                boolean: 1
            },
            prefix = (Math.random() + "_").slice(2);
        return {
            set: function (name, value) {
                if (this.isDefined(name)) {
                    return false;
                }
                if (!ownProp.call(allowed, typeof value)) {
                    return false;
                }
                constants[prefix + name] = value;
                return true;
            },
            isDefined: function (name) {
                return ownProp.call(constants, prefix + name);
            },
            get: function (name) {
                if (this.isDefined(name)) {
                    return constants[prefix + name];
                }
                return null;
            }
        };
    }());
```

Testing the implementation:

```
// check if defined
constant.isDefined("max_width"); // false

// define
constant.set("max_width", 480); // true

// check again
constant.isDefined("max_width"); // true

// attempt to redefine
constant.set("max_width", 320); // false

// is the value still intact?
constant.get("max_width"); // 480
```

Chaining Pattern

The chaining pattern enables you to call methods on an object one after the other, without assigning the return values of the previous operations to variables and without having to split your calls on multiple lines:

```
myobj.method1("hello").method2().method3("world").method4();
```

When you create methods that have no meaningful return value, you can have them return this, the instance of the object they are working with. This will enable consumers of that object to call the next method chained to the previous:

```
var obj = {
    value: 1,
    increment: function () {
        this.value += 1;
        return this;
    },
    add: function (v) {
        this.value += v;
        return this;
    },
    shout: function () {
        alert(this.value);
    }
};

// chain method calls
obj.increment().add(3).shout(); // 5

// as opposed to calling them one by one
obj.increment();
obj.add(3);
obj.shout(); // 5
```

Pros and Cons of the Chaining Pattern

A benefit of using the chaining pattern is that you can save some typing and create more concise code that almost reads like a sentence.

Another benefit is that it helps you think about splitting your functions and creating smaller, more specialized functions, as opposed to functions that try to do too much. This improves the maintainability in the long run.

A drawback is that it gets harder to debug code written this way. You may know that an error occurs on a specific line, but there's just too much going on in this line. When one of the several methods you've chained fails silently, you have no idea which one. Robert Martin, author of the book *Clean Code*, goes so far as to call this a "train wreck" pattern.

In any event, it's good to recognize this pattern, and when a method you write has no obvious and meaningful return value, you can always return this. The pattern is widely used, for example, in the jQuery library. And if you look at the DOM API, you can notice that it's also prone to chaining with constructs such as:

```
document.getElementsByTagName('head')[0].appendChild(newnode);
```

method() Method

JavaScript could be confusing to programmers who are used to thinking in terms of classes. That's why some developers opt to make JavaScript more class-like. One such attempt is the idea of the method() method introduced by Douglas Crockford. In retrospect, he admits that making JavaScript class-like is not a recommended approach, but nevertheless it's an interesting pattern, and you might come across it in some applications.

Using constructor functions looks like using classes in Java. They also enable you to add instance properties to this inside of the constructor body. However, adding methods to this is inefficient, because they end up being re-created with every instance and that consumes more memory. That's why reusable methods should be added to the prototype property of the constructor. The prototype may look alien to many developers, so you can hide it behind a method.

 Adding convenient functionality to a language is often referred to as *syntactic sugar* or simply *sugar*. In this case, you could call the method() method a "sugar method."

The way to define a "class" using the sugar method() would look like the following:

```
var Person = function (name) {
    this.name = name;
}.
    method('getName', function () {
        return this.name;
    }).
    method('setName', function (name) {
        this.name = name;
        return this;
    });
```

Note how the constructor is chained to the call to method(), which is in turn chained to the next method() call and so on. This follows the chaining pattern previously described and helps you define the whole "class" with a single statement.

The method() takes two parameters:

- The name of the new method
- The implementation of the method

This new method is then added to the Person "class." The implementation is just another function, and inside the implementation function this points to the object created by Person, as you would expect.

Here's how you can use `Person()` to create and use a new object:

```
var a = new Person('Adam');
a.getName(); // 'Adam'
a.setName('Eve').getName(); // 'Eve'
```

Again, note the chaining pattern in action, made possible simply because `setName()` returned `this`.

And finally, here's how the `method()` method is implemented:

```
if (typeof Function.prototype.method !== "function") {
    Function.prototype.method = function (name, implementation) {
        this.prototype[name] = implementation;
        return this;
    };
}
```

In this snippet, first we do the due diligence of checking whether `method()` doesn't already exist on `Function.prototype`. If not, we proceed with adding it. Then the job of the `method()` is to take the function passed as the argument `implementation` and add it to the prototype of the constructor. Here `this` refers to the constructor function, the prototype of which is augmented.

Summary

In this chapter you learned about different patterns to create objects that go beyond the basic patterns of using object literals and constructor functions.

You learned about the *namespacing* pattern that keeps the global space clean and helps organize and structure the code. You also learned about the simple, yet surprisingly helpful pattern of *declaring dependencies*. Then there was a detailed discussion on privacy patterns including *private* members, *privileged* methods, some edge cases with privacy, the use of object literals with private members, and *revealing* private methods as public ones. All these patterns are the building blocks for the popular and powerful *module pattern*.

Then you learned about the *sandbox pattern* as an alternative to the long namespacing, which also helps you create independent environments for your code and modules.

To wrap up the discussion, we took a deep look into *object constants*, *static methods* (both public and private), *chaining*, and a curious `method()` method.

CHAPTER 6

Code Reuse Patterns

Code reuse is an important and interesting topic simply because it's natural to strive for writing as little and reusing as much as possible from existing code, which you or someone else has already written. Especially if it's good, tested, maintainable, extensible, and documented code.

When talking about code reuse, the first thing that comes to mind is inheritance, and a great deal of the chapter is dedicated to this topic. You see several ways to do "classical" and nonclassical inheritance. But it's important to keep the end *goal* in mind—we want to reuse code. Inheritance is one way (*means*) for us to reach that goal. And it's not the only way. You see how you can compose objects from other objects, how to use object mix-ins, and how you can borrow and reuse only the functionality you need without technically inheriting anything permanently.

When approaching a code reuse task, keep in mind the advice the Gang of Four book has to offer on object creation: "Prefer object composition to class inheritance."

Classical Versus Modern Inheritance Patterns

Often you hear the term "classical inheritance" in discussions on the topic of inheritance in JavaScript, so let's first clarify what *classical* means. The term is not used in the sense of something antique, settled, or widely accepted as the proper way of doing things. The term is just a play on the word "class."

Many programming languages have the notion of classes as blueprints for objects. In those languages every object is an *instance* of a specific class and (in the case of Java, for example) an object cannot be created if the class for it doesn't exist. In JavaScript, because there are no classes, the notion of instances of classes doesn't make much sense. Objects in JavaScript are simply key-value pairs, which you can create and change on the fly.

But JavaScript has constructor functions, and the syntax of the new operator resembles a lot the syntax of using classes.

In Java you could do something like:

```
Person adam = new Person();
```

In JavaScript you would do:

```
var adam = new Person();
```

Other than the fact that Java is strongly typed and you need to declare that adam is of type Person, the syntax looks the same. JavaScript's constructor invocation looks as if Person were a class, but it's important to keep in mind that Person is still just a function. The similarity in syntax has led many developers to think about JavaScript in terms of classes and to develop ideas and inheritance patterns that assume classes. Such implementations we can call "classical." Let's also say that "modern" are any other patterns that do not require you to think about classes.

When it comes to adopting an inheritance pattern for your project, you have quite a few options. You should always strive for picking a modern pattern, unless the team is really uncomfortable if there are no classes involved.

This chapter discusses classical patterns first and then moves on to the modern ones.

Expected Outcome When Using Classical Inheritance

The goal of implementing classical inheritance is to have objects created by one constructor function Child() get properties that come from another constructor Parent().

 Although the discussion is about classical patterns, let's avoid using the word "class." Saying "constructor function" or "constructor" is longer, but it's accurate and not ambiguous. In general, strive for eliminating the word "class" when communicating within your team, because when it comes to JavaScript, the word may mean different things to different people.

Here's an example of defining the two constructors Parent() and Child():

```
// the parent constructor
function Parent(name) {
    this.name = name || 'Adam';
}

// adding functionality to the prototype
Parent.prototype.say = function () {
    return this.name;
};

// empty child constructor
function Child(name) {}
```

```
// inheritance magic happens here
inherit(Child, Parent);
```

Here you have the parent and child constructors, a method `say()` added to the parent constructor's prototype, and a call to a function called `inherit()` that takes care of the inheritance. The `inherit()` function is not provided by the language, so you have to implement it yourself. Let's see several approaches to implementing it in a generic way.

Classical Pattern #1—The Default Pattern

The default method most commonly used is to create an object using the `Parent()` constructor and assign this object to the `Child()`'s prototype. Here's the first implementation of the reusable `inherit()` function:

```
function inherit(C, P) {
    C.prototype = new P();
}
```

It's important to remember that the `prototype` property should point to an object, not a function, so it has to point to an instance (an object) created with the parent constructor, not to the constructor itself. In other words, pay attention to the new operator, because you need it for this pattern to work.

Later in your application when you use `new Child()` to create an object, it gets functionality from the `Parent()` instance via the prototype, as shown in the following example:

```
var kid = new Child();
kid.say(); // "Adam"
```

Following the Prototype Chain

Using this pattern you inherit both own properties (instance-specific properties added to this, such as name) and prototype properties and methods (such as `say()`).

Let's review how the prototype chain works in this inheritance pattern. For the purposes of this discussion, let's think of the objects as blocks somewhere in memory, which can contain data and references to other blocks. When you create an object using `new Parent()`, you create one such block (marked block #2 on Figure 6-1). It holds the data for the name property. If you attempt to access the `say()` method, though (for example, using `(new Parent).say()`), block #2 doesn't contain that method. But using the hidden link __proto__ that points to the `prototype` property of the constructor function `Parent()`, you gain access to object #1 (`Parent.prototype`), which does know about the `say()` method. All that happens behind the scenes and you don't need to worry about it, but it's important to know how it works and where the data you're accessing or maybe modifying is. Note that __proto__ is used here to explain the prototype chain; this property is not available in the language itself, although it's provided in some environments (for example, Firefox).

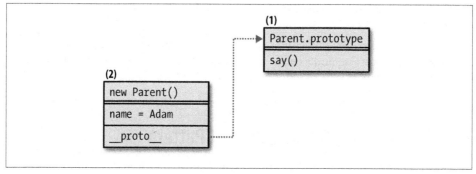

Figure 6-1. Prototype chain for the Parent() constructor

Now let's see what happens when a new object is created using var kid = new Child() after using the inherit() function. The diagram is shown on Figure 6-2.

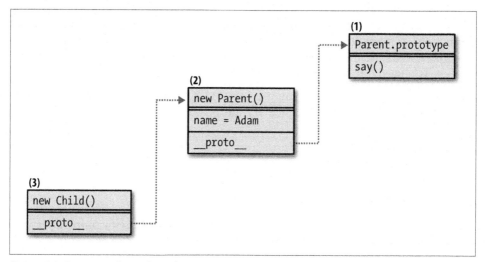

Figure 6-2. Prototype chain after inheritance

The Child() constructor was empty and no properties were added to Child.prototype; therefore, using new Child() creates objects that are pretty much empty, except for the hidden link __proto__. In this case, __proto__ points to the new Parent() object created in the inherit() function.

Now what happens when you do kid.say()? Object #3 doesn't have such a method, so it looks up to #2 via the prototype chain. Object #2 doesn't have it either, so it follows the chain up to #1, which does happen to have it. Then inside say() there's a reference to this.name, which needs to be resolved. The lookup starts again. In this case, this points to object #3, which doesn't have name. Object #2 is consulted and it does have a name property, with the value "Adam."

Finally, let's take a look at one more step. Let's say we have this code:

```
var kid = new Child();
kid.name = "Patrick";
kid.say(); // "Patrick"
```

Figure 6-3 shows how the chain will look in this case.

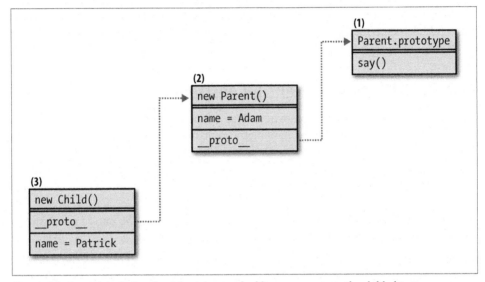

Figure 6-3. Prototype chain after inheritance and adding a property to the child object

Setting the `kid.name` doesn't change the `name` property of object #2, but it creates an own property directly on the `kid` object #3. When you do `kid.say()`, the method `say` is looked up in object #3, then #2, and then finally found in #1, just as before. But this time looking up `this.name` (which is the same as `kid.name`) is quick, because the property is found right away in object #3.

If you remove the new property using `delete kid.name`, then the `name` property of object #2 will "shine through" and be found in consecutive lookups.

Drawbacks When Using Pattern #1

One drawback of this pattern is that you inherit both own properties added to this and prototype properties. Most of the time you don't want the own properties, because they are likely to be specific to one instance and not reusable.

A general rule of thumb with constructors is that the reusable members should be added to the prototype.

Another thing about using a generic `inherit()` function is that it doesn't enable you to pass parameters to the child constructor, which the child then passes to the parent. Consider this example:

```
var s = new Child('Seth');
s.say(); // "Adam"
```

This is not what you'd expect. It's possible for the child to pass parameters to the parent's constructor, but then you have to do the inheritance every time you need a new child, which is inefficient, because you end up re-creating parent objects over and over.

Classical Pattern #2—Rent-a-Constructor

This next pattern solves the problem of passing arguments from the child to the parent. It borrows the parent constructor, passing the child object to be bound to `this` and also forwarding any arguments:

```
function Child(a, c, b, d) {
    Parent.apply(this, arguments);
}
```

This way you can only inherit properties added to `this` inside the parent constructor. You don't inherit members that were added to the prototype.

Using the borrowed constructor pattern, the children objects get copies of the inherited members, unlike the classical #1 pattern where they only get references. The following example illustrates the difference:

```
// a parent constructor
function Article() {
    this.tags = ['js', 'css'];
}
var article = new Article();

// a blog post inherits from an article object
// via the classical pattern #1
function BlogPost() {}
BlogPost.prototype = article;
var blog = new BlogPost();
// note that above you didn't need `new Article()`
// because you already had an instance available

// a static page inherits from article
// via the rented constructor pattern
function StaticPage() {
    Article.call(this);
}
var page = new StaticPage();

alert(article.hasOwnProperty('tags')); // true
alert(blog.hasOwnProperty('tags')); // false
alert(page.hasOwnProperty('tags')); // true
```

In this snippet, the parent `Article()` is inherited in two ways. The default pattern causes the `blog` object to gain access to the `tags` property via the prototype, so it doesn't have it as an own property and `hasOwnProperty()` returns `false`. The `page` object has an own `tags` property because using the rented constructor the new object got a copy of (not a reference to) the parent's `tags` member.

Note the difference when modifying the inherited `tags` property:

```
blog.tags.push('html');
page.tags.push('php');
alert(article.tags.join(', ')); // "js, css, html"
```

In this example the child `blog` object modifies the `tags` property, and this way it also modifies the parent because essentially both `blog.tags` and `article.tags` point to the same array. Changes to `page.tags` don't affect the parent article because `page.tags` is a separate copy created during inheritance.

The Prototype Chain

Let's take a look at how the prototype chain looks when using this pattern and the familiar `Parent()` and `Child()` constructors. `Child()` will be slightly modified to follow the new pattern:

```
// the parent constructor
function Parent(name) {
    this.name = name || 'Adam';
}

// adding functionality to the prototype
Parent.prototype.say = function () {
    return this.name;
};

// child constructor
function Child(name) {
    Parent.apply(this, arguments);
}

var kid = new Child("Patrick");
kid.name; // "Patrick"
typeof kid.say; // "undefined"
```

If you take a look at Figure 6-4, you'll notice that there's no longer a link between the new `Child` object and the `Parent`. That's because `Child.prototype` was not used at all, and it simply points to a blank object. Using this pattern, `kid` got its own property name, but the `say()` method was never inherited, and an attempt to call it will result in an error. The inheritance was a one-off action that copied parent's own properties as child's own properties and that was about it; no __proto__ links were kept.

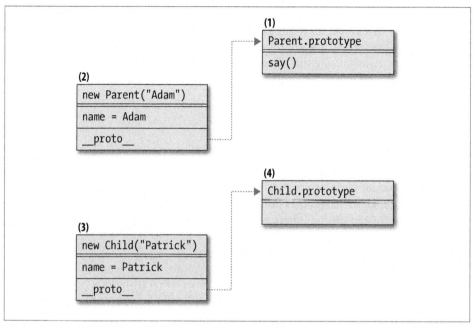

Figure 6-4. The broken chain when using the borrowing constructor pattern

Multiple Inheritance by Borrowing Constructors

Using the borrowing constructors patterns, it's possible to implement multiple inheritance simply by borrowing from more than one constructor:

```
function Cat() {
    this.legs = 4;
    this.say = function () {
        return "meaowww";
    }
}

function Bird() {
    this.wings = 2;
    this.fly = true;
}

function CatWings() {
    Cat.apply(this);
    Bird.apply(this);
}

var jane = new CatWings();
console.dir(jane);
```

The result is shown in Figure 6-5. Any duplicate properties will be resolved by having the last one win.

fly	true
legs	4
wings	2
say	function()

Figure 6-5. A CatWings object inspected in Firebug

Pros and Cons of the Borrowing Constructor Pattern

The drawback of this pattern is obviously that nothing from the prototype gets inherited and, as mentioned before, the prototype is the place to add reusable methods and properties, which will not be re-created for every instance.

A benefit is that you get true copies of the parent's own members, and there's no risk that a child can accidentally overwrite a parent's property.

So how can the children inherit prototype properties too, in the previous case, and how can kid get access to the **say()** method? The next pattern addresses this question.

Classical Pattern #3—Rent and Set Prototype

Combining the previous two patterns, you first borrow the constructor and then also set the child's prototype to point to a new instance of the constructor:

```
function Child(a, c, b, d) {
    Parent.apply(this, arguments);
}
Child.prototype = new Parent();
```

The benefit is that the result objects get copies of the parent's own members and references to the parent's reusable functionality (implemented as members of the prototype). The child can also pass any arguments to the parent constructor. This behavior is probably the closest to what you'd expect in Java; you inherit everything there is in the parent, and at the same time it's safe to modify own properties without the risk of modifying the parent.

A drawback is that the parent constructor is called twice, so it could be inefficient. At the end, the own properties (such as name in our case) get inherited twice.

Let's take a look at the code and do some testing:

```
// the parent constructor
function Parent(name) {
    this.name = name || 'Adam';
}

// adding functionality to the prototype
Parent.prototype.say = function () {
    return this.name;
```

```
};

// child constructor
function Child(name) {
    Parent.apply(this, arguments);
}
Child.prototype = new Parent();

var kid = new Child("Patrick");
kid.name; // "Patrick"
kid.say(); // "Patrick"
delete kid.name;
kid.say(); // "Adam"
```

Unlike the previous pattern, now say() is inherited properly. You can also notice that name is inherited two times, and after we delete the own copy, the one that comes down the prototype chain will shine through.

Figure 6-6 shows how the relationships between the objects work. The relationships are similar to those shown in Figure 6-3, but the way we got there was different.

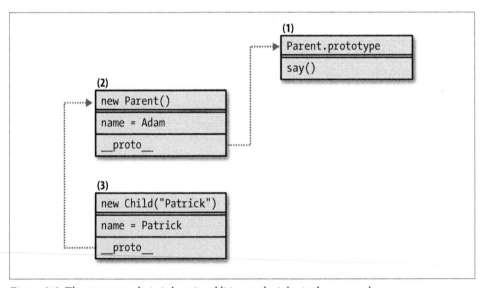

Figure 6-6. The prototype chain is kept in addition to the inherited own members

Classical Pattern #4—Share the Prototype

Unlike the previous classical inheritance pattern, which required two calls to the parent constructor, the next pattern doesn't involve calling the parent constructor at all.

The rule of thumb was that reusable members should go to the prototype and not this. Therefore for inheritance purposes, anything worth inheriting should be in the prototype. So you can just set the child's prototype to be the same as the parent's prototype:

```
function inherit(C, P) {
    C.prototype = P.prototype;
}
```

This gives you short and fast prototype chain lookups because all objects actually share the same prototype. But that's also a drawback because if one child or grandchild somewhere down the inheritance chain modifies the prototype, it affects all parents and grandparents.

As Figure 6-7 shows, both child and parent objects share the same prototype and get equal access to the say() method. However, children objects don't inherit the name property.

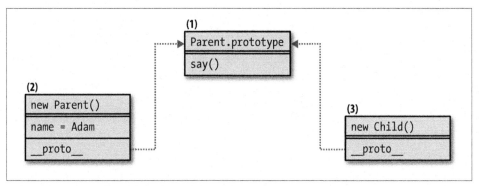

Figure 6-7. Relationships when sharing the same prototype

Classical Pattern #5—A Temporary Constructor

The next pattern solves the same-prototype problem by breaking the direct link between parent's and child's prototype while at the same time benefiting from the prototype chain.

Below is an implementation of this pattern, where you have an empty function F(), which serves as a proxy between the child and the parent. F()'s prototype property points to the prototype of the parent. The prototype of the child is an instance of the blank function:

```
function inherit(C, P) {
    var F = function () {};
    F.prototype = P.prototype;
    C.prototype = new F();
}
```

This pattern has a behavior slightly different from the default pattern (classical pattern #1) because here the child only inherits properties of the prototype (see Figure 6-8).

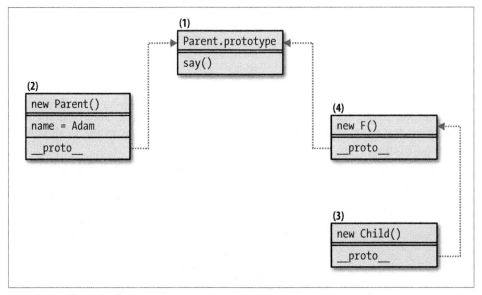

Figure 6-8. Classical inheritance by using a temporary (proxy) constructor F()

And that's usually fine, actually preferable, because the prototype is the place for reusable functionality. In this pattern, any members that the parent constructor adds to `this` are not inherited.

Let's create a new child object and inspect its behavior:

```
var kid = new Child();
```

If you access `kid.name` it will be `undefined`. In this case `name` is an own property of the parent, and while inheriting we actually never called `new Parent()`, so this property was never even created. When you access `kid.say()`, it won't be available in object #3, so the prototype chain is looked up. Object #4 doesn't have this method either, but object #1 does and this is the same location in memory, which will be reused by all different constructors that inherit `Parent()` and all the objects created by all the children.

Storing the Superclass

Building on top of the previous pattern, you can add a reference to the original parent. This is like having access to the superclass in other languages and could be handy on occasion.

The property is called `uber` because "super" is a reserved word and "superclass" may lead the unsuspecting developer down the path of thinking that JavaScript has classes. Here's an improved implementation of this classical pattern:

```
function inherit(C, P) {
    var F = function () {};
    F.prototype = P.prototype;
    C.prototype = new F();
    C.uber = P.prototype;
}
```

Resetting the Constructor Pointer

One last thing to add to this almost perfect classical inheritance function is to reset the pointer to the constructor function in case you need it down the road.

If you don't reset the pointer to the constructor, then all children objects will report that Parent() was their constructor, which is not useful. So using the previous implementation of inherit(), you can observe this behavior:

```
// parent, child, inheritance
function Parent() {}
function Child() {}
inherit(Child, Parent);

// testing the waters
var kid = new Child();
kid.constructor.name; // "Parent"
kid.constructor === Parent; // true
```

The constructor property is rarely used but could be convenient for runtime introspection of objects. You can reset it to point to the expected constructor function without affecting the functionality because this property is mostly informational.

The final Holy Grail version of this classical inheritance pattern will look like so:

```
function inherit(C, P) {
    var F = function () {};
    F.prototype = P.prototype;
    C.prototype = new F();
    C.uber = P.prototype;
    C.prototype.constructor = C;
}
```

A function similar to this exists in the YUI library (and probably other libraries) and brings the classical inheritance to a language without classes, if you decide that this is the best approach for your project.

 This pattern is also referred to as one using a *proxy function* or a *proxy constructor*, instead of a *temporary constructor*, because the temporary constructor is used as a proxy to get to the parent's prototype.

A common optimization of the Holy Grail pattern is to avoid creating the temporary (proxy) constructor every time you need inheritance. It's sufficient to create it once and only change its prototype. You can use an immediate function and store the proxy function in its closure:

```
var inherit = (function () {
    var F = function () {};
    return function (C, P) {
        F.prototype = P.prototype;
        C.prototype = new F();
        C.uber = P.prototype;
        C.prototype.constructor = C;
    }
}());
```

Klass

Many JavaScript libraries emulate classes, introducing new sugar syntax. The implementations differ but there are often some commonalities, including the following:

- There's a convention on how to name a method, which is to be considered the constructor of the class, for example `initialize`, `_init`, or something similar and which gets called automatically.
- Classes inherit from other classes.
- There's access to the parent class (superclass) from within the child class.

 Let's shift gears here and, in this part of the chapter only, use the word "class" freely because the topic is emulating classes.

Without going into too much detail, let's see an example implementation of simulated classes in JavaScript. First, how will the solution be used from the client's perspective?

```
var Man = klass(null, {
    __construct: function (what) {
        console.log("Man's constructor");
        this.name = what;
    },
    getName: function () {
        return this.name;
    }
});
```

The syntax sugar comes in the form of a function called `klass()`. In some implementations you may see it as `Klass()` constructor or as augmented `Object.prototype`, but in this example, let's keep it a simple function.

The function takes two parameters: a parent class to be inherited and implementation of the new class provided by an object literal. Influenced by PHP, let's establish the convention that the class's constructor must be a method called `__construct`. In the preceding snippet, a new class called Man is created and doesn't inherit from anything (which means inherit from Object behind the scenes). The Man class has an own property name created inside __construct and a method getName(). The class is a constructor function, so the following will still work (and will look just like a class instantiation):

```
var first = new Man('Adam'); // logs "Man's constructor"
first.getName(); // "Adam"
```

Now let's extend this class and create a SuperMan class:

```
var SuperMan = klass(Man, {
    __construct: function (what) {
        console.log("SuperMan's constructor");
    },
    getName: function () {
        var name = SuperMan.uber.getName.call(this);
        return "I am " + name;
    }
});
```

Here, the first parameter to klass() is the class Man to be inherited. Notice also in getName() that the parent class's getName() function is called first by using the uber (super) static property of SuperMan. Let's test:

```
var clark = new SuperMan('Clark Kent');
clark.getName(); // "I am Clark Kent"
```

The first line logs to the console "Man's constructor" and then "Superman's constructor." In some languages the parent's constructor is called automatically every time the child's constructor is called, so why not emulate that as well?

Testing that instanceof operator returns expected results:

```
clark instanceof Man; // true
clark instanceof SuperMan; // true
```

Finally, let's see how the klass() function can be implemented:

```
var klass = function (Parent, props) {

    var Child, F, i;

    // 1.
    // new constructor
    Child = function () {
        if (Child.uber && Child.uber.hasOwnProperty("__construct")) {
            Child.uber.__construct.apply(this, arguments);
        }
        if (Child.prototype.hasOwnProperty("__construct")) {
            Child.prototype.__construct.apply(this, arguments);
        }
    };

    // 2.
    // inherit
    Parent = Parent || Object;
```

```
        F = function () {};
        F.prototype = Parent.prototype;
        Child.prototype = new F();
        Child.uber = Parent.prototype;
        Child.prototype.constructor = Child;

        // 3.
        // add implementation methods
        for (i in props) {
            if (props.hasOwnProperty(i)) {
                Child.prototype[i] = props[i];
            }
        }

        // return the "class"
        return Child;
    };
```

The klass() implementation has three interesting and distinct parts:

1. A Child() constructor function is created. This is the function that will be returned at the end and will be used as a class. In this function the __construct method is called if it exists. Also before that the parent's __construct is called (again, if it exists) using the static uber property. There might be cases when uber is not defined—when you inherit from Object for example, as the case was with the Man class definition.

2. The second part takes care of the inheritance bit. It's simply using the classical inheritance's Holy Grail pattern discussed in the previous section of the chapter. There's only one new thing: setting the Parent to Object if no Parent was passed to inherit from.

3. The final section is looping through all the implementation methods (such as __construct and getName in the examples), which are the actual definition of the class and adding them to the prototype of Child.

When to use such a pattern? Well, it's actually better if you avoid it, because it brings the whole confusing notion of classes, which don't technically exist in the language. It adds new syntax and new rules to learn and remember. That said, if you or the team feel at ease with classes and at the same time feel uncomfortable with prototypes, then this could be something to explore. This pattern allows you to forget about the prototypes completely, and the good thing is you can tweak the syntax and the conventions to resemble another of your favorite languages.

Prototypal Inheritance

Let's start the discussion of "modern" classless patterns with a pattern called *prototypal inheritance*. In this pattern there are no classes involved; here objects inherit from other objects. You can think about it this way: you have an object that you would like to reuse and you want to create a second object that gets its functionality from the first one.

Here's how you would go about this:

```
// object to inherit from
var parent = {
    name: "Papa"
};

// the new object
var child = object(parent);

// testing
alert(child.name); // "Papa"
```

In the preceding snippet, you have an existing object called `parent` created with the object literal, and you want to create another object called `child` that has the same properties and methods as the parent. The `child` object was created with a function called `object()`. This function doesn't exist in JavaScript (not to be mistaken with the constructor function `Object()`), so let's see how you can define it.

Similarly to the classical Holy Grail, you would use an empty temporary constructor function `F()`. You then set the prototype of `F()` to be the parent object. Finally, you return a new instance of the temporary constructor:

```
function object(o) {
    function F() {}
    F.prototype = o;
    return new F();
}
```

Figure 6-9 shows the prototype chain when using the prototypal inheritance pattern. Here `child` always starts as an empty object, which has no properties of its own but at the same time has all the functionality of its parent by benefiting from the __proto__ link.

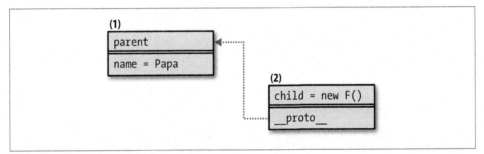

Figure 6-9. Prototypal inheritance pattern

Discussion

In the prototypal inheritance pattern, your parent doesn't need to be created with the literal notation (although that is probably the more common way). You can have constructor functions create the parent. Note that if you do so, both "own" properties and properties of the constructor's prototype will be inherited:

```
// parent constructor
function Person() {
    // an "own" property
    this.name = "Adam";
}
// a property added to the prototype
Person.prototype.getName = function () {
    return this.name;
};

// create a new person
var papa = new Person();
// inherit
var kid = object(papa);

// test that both the own property
// and the prototype property were inherited
kid.getName(); // "Adam"
```

In another variation of this pattern you have the option to inherit just the prototype object of an existing constructor. Remember, objects inherit from objects, regardless of how the parent objects were created. Here's an illustration using the previous example, slightly modified:

```
// parent constructor
function Person() {
    // an "own" property
    this.name = "Adam";
}
// a property added to the prototype
Person.prototype.getName = function () {
    return this.name;
};

// inherit
var kid = object(Person.prototype);

typeof kid.getName; // "function", because it was in the prototype
typeof kid.name; // "undefined", because only the prototype was inherited
```

Addition to ECMAScript 5

In ECMAScript 5, the prototypal inheritance pattern becomes officially a part of the language. This pattern is implemented through the method Object.create(). In other words, you won't need to roll your own function similar to `object()`; it will be built into the language:

```
var child = Object.create(parent);
```

`Object.create()` accepts an additional parameter, an object. The properties of the extra object will be added as own properties of the new child object being returned. This is a convenience that enables you to inherit and build upon the child object with one method call. For example:

```
var child = Object.create(parent, {
    age: { value: 2 } // ECMA5 descriptor
});
child.hasOwnProperty("age"); // true
```

You may also find that the prototypal inheritance pattern is implemented in JavaScript libraries; for example, in YUI3 it's the `Y.Object()` method:

```
YUI().use('*', function (Y) {
    var child = Y.Object(parent);
});
```

Inheritance by Copying Properties

Let's take a look at another inheritance pattern—inheritance by copying properties. In this pattern, an object gets functionality from another object, simply by copying it. Here's an example implementation of a sample function `extend()` that does that:

```
function extend(parent, child) {
    var i;
    child = child || {};
    for (i in parent) {
        if (parent.hasOwnProperty(i)) {
            child[i] = parent[i];
        }
    }
    return child;
}
```

It's a simple implementation, just looping through the parent's members and copying them over. In this implementation `child` is optional; if you don't pass an existing object to be augmented, then a brand new object is created and returned:

```
var dad = {name: "Adam"};
var kid = extend(dad);
kid.name; // "Adam"
```

The implementation given is a so-called "shallow copy" of the object. A deep copy on the other hand would mean checking if the property you're about to copy is an object or an array, and if so, recursively iterating through its properties and copying them as well. With the shallow copy (because objects are passed by reference in JavaScript), if you mutate a property of the child, and this property happens to be an object, then you'll be modifying the parent as well. This is actually preferable for methods (as functions are also objects and are passed by reference) but could lead to surprises when working with other objects and arrays. Consider this:

```
var dad = {
    counts: [1, 2, 3],
    reads: {paper: true}
};
var kid = extend(dad);
kid.counts.push(4);
dad.counts.toString(); // "1,2,3,4"
dad.reads === kid.reads; // true
```

Now let's modify the extend() function to make deep copies. All you need is to check if a property's type is an object, and if so, recursively copy its properties. Another check you need is if the object is a true object or if it's an array. Let's use the check for array-ness discussed in Chapter 3. So the deep copy version of extend() would look like so:

```
function extendDeep(parent, child) {
    var i,
        toStr = Object.prototype.toString,
        astr = "[object Array]";

    child = child || {};

    for (i in parent) {
        if (parent.hasOwnProperty(i)) {
            if (typeof parent[i] === "object") {
                child[i] = (toStr.call(parent[i]) === astr) ? [] : {};
                extendDeep(parent[i], child[i]);
            } else {
                child[i] = parent[i];
            }
        }
    }
    return child;
}
```

Now testing the new implementation gives us true copies of objects, so child objects don't modify their parents:

```
var dad = {
    counts: [1, 2, 3],
    reads: {paper: true}
};
var kid = extendDeep(dad);

kid.counts.push(4);
kid.counts.toString(); // "1,2,3,4"
dad.counts.toString(); // "1,2,3"

dad.reads === kid.reads; // false
kid.reads.paper = false;
```

```
    kid.reads.web = true;
    dad.reads.paper; // true
```

This property copying pattern is simple and widely used; for example, Firebug (Firefox extensions are written in JavaScript) has a method called extend() that makes shallow copies and jQuery's extend() creates a deep copy. YUI3 offers a method called Y.clone(), which creates a deep copy and also copies over functions by binding them to the child object. (There will be more on binding later in this chapter.)

It's worth noting that there are no prototypes involved in this pattern at all; it's only about objects and their own properties.

Mix-ins

Taking the idea of inheritance by property copying a step further, let's consider a "mix-in" pattern. Instead of copying from one object, you can copy from any number of objects and mix them all into a new object.

The implementation is simple; just loop through arguments and copy every property of every object passed to the function:

```
function mix() {
    var arg, prop, child = {};
    for (arg = 0; arg < arguments.length; arg += 1) {
        for (prop in arguments[arg]) {
            if (arguments[arg].hasOwnProperty(prop)) {
                child[prop] = arguments[arg][prop];
            }
        }
    }
    return child;
}
```

Now that you have a generic mix-in function, you can pass any number of objects to it, and the result will be a new object that has the properties of all the source objects. Here is an example use:

```
var cake = mix(
    {eggs: 2, large: true},
    {butter: 1, salted: true},
    {flour: "3 cups"},
    {sugar: "sure!"}
);
```

Figure 6-10 shows the result of displaying the properties of the new mixed-in cake objects by executing console.dir(cake) in the Firebug console.

butter	1
eggs	2
flour	"3 cups"
large	true
salted	true
sugar	"sure!"

Figure 6-10. Examining the cake object in Firebug

 If you're used to the mix-in concept from languages in which it's an official part of the language, you might expect that changing one or more of the parents will affect the child, but that's not true in the given implementation. Here we simply loop, copy own properties, and break the link with the parent(s).

Borrowing Methods

Sometimes it may happen that you only like one or two methods of an existing object. You want to reuse them, but you don't really want to form a parent-child relationship with that object. You want to use just the methods you like, without inheriting all the other methods that you'll never need. This is possible with the borrowing methods pattern, which benefits from the function methods `call()` and `apply()`. You've seen this pattern already in the book and even in this chapter in the implementation of `extendDeep()`, for example.

As you know, functions in JavaScript are objects, and they come with some interesting methods of their own, such as `call()` and `apply()`. The only difference between the two is that one takes an array of parameters to be passed to the method being called, and the other one takes parameters one by one. You can use these methods to borrow functionality from existing objects:

```
// call() example
notmyobj.doStuff.call(myobj, param1, p2, p3);
// apply() example
notmyobj.doStuff.apply(myobj, [param1, p2, p3]);
```

Here you have an object called `myobj` and you know that some other object called `notmyobj` has this useful method called `doStuff()`. Instead of going through the inheritance hassle and inheriting a number of methods your `myobj` will never need, you can simply borrow the method `doStuff()` temporarily.

You pass your object and any parameters, and the borrowed method binds your object as its own `this`. Basically, your object pretends to be the other object for a bit to benefit from the method you like. It's like getting an inheritance but without paying the inheritance tax (where the "tax" comes in the form of extra properties and methods you have no need for).

Example: Borrow from Array

A common use for this pattern is borrowing array methods.

Arrays have useful methods, which array-like objects such as `arguments` don't have. So `arguments` can borrow array methods, such as the method `slice()`. Here's one example:

```
function f() {
    var args = [].slice.call(arguments, 1, 3);
    return args;
}

// example
f(1, 2, 3, 4, 5, 6); // returns [2,3]
```

In this example, there's an empty array created just for the sake of using its method. A slightly longer way to do the same is to borrow the method directly from `Array`'s prototype, using `Array.prototype.slice.call(...)`. This way is a little longer to type, but you'll save the work of creating one empty array.

Borrow and Bind

When borrowing methods either through `call()`/`apply()` or through simple assignment, the object that `this` points to inside of the borrowed method is determined based on the call expression. But sometimes it's best to have the value of `this` "locked" or bound to a specific object and predetermined in advance.

Let's see an example. There's an object called `one` that has a `say()` method:

```
var one = {
    name: "object",
    say: function (greet) {
        return greet + ", " + this.name;
    }
};

// test
one.say('hi'); // "hi, object"
```

Now another object `two` doesn't have a `say()` method, but it can borrow it from `one`:

```
var two = {
    name: "another object"
};

one.say.apply(two, ['hello']); // "hello, another object"
```

In the preceding case, `this` inside `say()` pointed to `two` and `this.name` was therefore "another object." But what about scenarios in which you assign the function pointer to a global variable or you pass the function as a callback? In client-side programming there are a lot of events and callbacks, so that does happen a lot:

```
// assigning to a variable
// `this` will point to the global object
```

```
var say = one.say;
say('hoho'); // "hoho, undefined"

// passing as a callback
var yetanother = {
    name: "Yet another object",
    method: function (callback) {
        return callback('Hola');
    }
};
yetanother.method(one.say); // "Hola, undefined"
```

In both of those cases this inside say() was pointing to the global object, and the whole snippet didn't work as expected. To fix (in other words, bind) an object to a method, we can use a simple function like this:

```
function bind(o, m) {
    return function () {
        return m.apply(o, [].slice.call(arguments));
    };
}
```

This bind() function accepts an object o and a method m, binds the two together, and then returns another function. The returned function has access to o and m via a closure. Therefore even after bind() returns, the inner function will have access to o and m, which will always point to the original object and method. Let's create a new function using bind():

```
var twosay = bind(two, one.say);
twosay('yo'); // "yo, another object"
```

As you can see, even though twosay() was created as a global function, this didn't point to the global object, but it pointed to object two, which was passed to bind(). Regardless of how you call twosay(), this will always be bound to two.

The price you pay for the luxury of having a bind is the additional closure.

Function.prototype.bind()

ECMAScript 5 adds a method bind() to Function.prototype, making it just as easy to use as apply() and call(). So you can do expressions like:

```
var newFunc = obj.someFunc.bind(myobj, 1, 2, 3);
```

This means bind together someFunc() and myobj and also prefill the first three arguments that someFunc() expects. This is also an example of partial function application discussed in Chapter 4.

Let's see how you can implement Function.prototype.bind() when your program runs in pre-ES5 environments:

```
if (typeof Function.prototype.bind === "undefined") {
    Function.prototype.bind = function (thisArg) {
        var fn = this,
```

```
            slice = Array.prototype.slice,
            args = slice.call(arguments, 1);

        return function () {
            return fn.apply(thisArg, args.concat(slice.call(arguments)));
        };
    };
}
```

This implementation probably looks a bit familiar; it's using partial application and concatenating the list of arguments—those passed to bind() (except the first) and those passed when the new function returned by bind() is called later. Here's an example use:

```
var twosay2 = one.say.bind(two);
twosay2('Bonjour'); // "Bonjour, another object"
```

In the preceding example, we didn't pass any parameters to bind() other than the object to be bound. In the next example, let's pass an argument to be partially applied:

```
var twosay3 = one.say.bind(two, 'Enchanté');
twosay3(); // "Enchanté, another object"
```

Summary

There are many options available when it comes to inheritance in JavaScript. It's beneficial to study and understand the different patterns because they help improve your grasp of the language. In this chapter you learned about several classical and several modern patterns to approach inheritance.

However, inheritance is probably not a problem you face often during development. This is partially due to the fact that this problem is probably already solved in some way or another by the library you use—and partially because it's rare that you need to establish long and complicated inheritance chains in JavaScript. In static strongly typed languages, inheritance may be the only way to reuse code. In JavaScript you may often have much simpler and elegant ways, including borrowing methods, binding them, copying properties, and mixing-in properties from several objects.

Remember that code reuse is the goal, and inheritance is just one of the ways to accomplish that goal.

CHAPTER 7

Design Patterns

The design patterns from the Gang of Four book offer solutions to common problems related to the object-oriented software design. They have been around for quite a while and have been proven useful in many situations. That's why it's good to familiarize yourself with them and to talk about them.

Although these design patterns are language-independent and implementation-agnostic, they have been studied for many years, mainly from the perspective of strongly typed static-class languages, such as C++ and Java.

JavaScript, being an untyped dynamic prototype-based language, sometimes makes it surprisingly easy, even trivial, to implement some of these patterns.

Let's start with the first example of how things are different in JavaScript compared to a static class-based language—the singleton pattern.

Singleton

The idea of the singleton pattern is to have only one instance of a specific class. This means that the second time you use the same class to create a new object, you should get the same object that was created the first time.

And how does this apply to JavaScript? In JavaScript there are no classes, just objects. When you create a new object, there's actually no other object like it, and the new object is already a singleton. Creating a simple object using the object literal is also an example of a singleton:

```
var obj = {
    myprop: 'my value'
};
```

In JavaScript, objects are never equal unless they are the same object, so even if you create an identical object with the exact same members, it won't be the same as the first one:

```
var obj2 = {
    myprop: 'my value'
};
obj === obj2; // false
obj == obj2;  // false
```

So you can say that every time you create an object using the object literal, you're actually creating a singleton, and there's no special syntax involved.

Note that sometimes when people say "singleton" in a JavaScript context, they mean the module pattern discussed in Chapter 5.

Using new

JavaScript doesn't have classes, so the verbatim definition for singleton doesn't technically make sense. But JavaScript has the new syntax for creating objects using constructor functions, and sometimes you might want a singleton implementation using this syntax. The idea is that when you use new to create several objects using the same constructor, you should get only new pointers to the exact same object.

Usefulness warning: The following discussion is not so useful as a practical pattern but more as a theoretical exercise in imitating the workarounds for issues related to the designs of some (statically, strongly typed) class-based languages in which functions are not first-class objects.

The following snippet shows the expected behavior (assuming that you dismiss the idea of the Multiverse and accept that there's only one Universe out there):

```
var uni  = new Universe();
var uni2 = new Universe();
uni === uni2; // true
```

In this example, uni is created only the first time the constructor is called. The second time (and the third, fourth, and so on) the same uni object is returned. This is why uni === uni2—because they are essentially two references pointing to the exact same object. And how to achieve this in JavaScript?

You need your Universe constructor to cache the object instance this when it's created and then return it the second time the constructor is called. You have several options to achieve this:

- You can use a global variable to store the instance. This is not recommended because of the general principle that globals are bad. Plus, anyone can overwrite this global variable, even by accident. So let's not discuss this option any further.

- You can cache in a static property of the constructor. Functions in JavaScript are objects, so they can have properties. You can have something like `Universe.instance` and cache the object there. This is a nice, clean solution with the only drawback that the `instance` property is publicly accessible, and code outside of yours might change it, so you lose the instance.

- You can wrap the instance in a closure. This keeps the instance private and not available for modifications outside of your constructor at the expense of an extra closure.

Let's take a look at an example implementation of the second and third options.

Instance in a Static Property

Here's an example of caching the singular instance in a static property of the Universe constructor:

```
function Universe() {

    // do we have an existing instance?
    if (typeof Universe.instance === "object") {
        return Universe.instance;
    }

    // proceed as normal
    this.start_time = 0;
    this.bang = "Big";

    // cache
    Universe.instance = this;

    // implicit return:
    // return this;
}

// testing
var uni  = new Universe();
var uni2 = new Universe();
uni === uni2; // true
```

As you see, this is a straightforward solution with the only drawback that `instance` is public. It's unlikely that other code will change it by mistake (much less likely than if `instance` was a global) but still possible.

Instance in a Closure

Another way to do the class-like singleton is to use a closure to protect the single instance. You can implement this by using the private static member pattern discussed
in Chapter 5. The secret sauce here is to rewrite the constructor:

```
function Universe() {

    // the cached instance
    var instance = this;

    // proceed as normal
    this.start_time = 0;
    this.bang = "Big";

    // rewrite the constructor
    Universe = function () {
        return instance;
    };
}

// testing
var uni  = new Universe();
var uni2 = new Universe();
uni === uni2; // true
```

The original constructor is called the first time and it returns this as usual. Then the
second, third time, and so on the rewritten constructor is executed. The rewritten constructor has access to the private instance variable via the closure and simply returns it.

This implementation is actually another example of the self-defining function pattern
from Chapter 4. The drawback, as we discussed there, is that the rewritten function
(in this case the constructor Universe()) will lose any properties added to it between
the moment of initial definition and the redefinition. In our specific case anything you
add to the prototype of Universe() will not have a live link to the instance created with
the original implementation.

Here's how you can see the problem with some testing:

```
// adding to the prototype
Universe.prototype.nothing = true;

var uni  = new Universe();

// again adding to the prototype
// after the initial object is created
Universe.prototype.everything = true;

var uni2 = new Universe();
```

Testing:

```
// only the original prototype was
// linked to the objects
```

```
uni.nothing; // true
uni2.nothing; // true
uni.everything; // undefined
uni2.everything; // undefined

// that sounds right:
uni.constructor.name; // "Universe"

// but that's odd:
uni.constructor === Universe; // false
```

The reason that uni.constructor is no longer the same as the Universe() constructor is because uni.constructor still points to the original constructor, not the redefined one.

If getting the prototype and the constructor pointer working as expected is a requirement, it's possible to achieve this with a few tweaks:

```
function Universe() {

    // the cached instance
    var instance;

    // rewrite the constructor
    Universe = function Universe() {
        return instance;
    };

    // carry over the prototype properties
    Universe.prototype = this;

    // the instance
    instance = new Universe();

    // reset the constructor pointer
    instance.constructor = Universe;

    // all the functionality
    instance.start_time = 0;
    instance.bang = "Big";

    return instance;
}
```

Now all the test cases should work as expected:

```
// update prototype and create instance
Universe.prototype.nothing = true; // true
var uni = new Universe();
Universe.prototype.everything = true; // true
var uni2 = new Universe();

// it's the same single instance
uni === uni2; // true

// all prototype properties work
// no matter when they were defined
```

```
uni.nothing && uni.everything && uni2.nothing && uni2.everything; // true
// the normal properties work
uni.bang; // "Big"
// the constructor points correctly
uni.constructor === Universe; // true
```

An alternative solution would also be to wrap the constructor and the instance in an immediate function. The first time the constructor is invoked, it creates an object and also points the private `instance` to it. From the second invocation on, the constructor simply returns the private variable. All the tests from the previous snippet will work as expected, too, with this new implementation:

```
var Universe;

(function () {

    var instance;

    Universe = function Universe() {

        if (instance) {
            return instance;
        }

        instance = this;

        // all the functionality
        this.start_time = 0;
        this.bang = "Big";

    };

}());
```

Factory

The purpose of the factory is to create objects. It's usually implemented in a class or a static method of a class, which has the following purposes:

- Performs repeating operations when setting up similar objects
- Offers a way for the customers of the factory to create objects without knowing the specific type (class) at compile time

The second point is more important in static class languages in which it may be non-trivial to create instances of classes, which are not known in advance (in compile time). In JavaScript, this part of the implementation is quite easy.

The objects created by the factory method (or class) are by design inheriting from the same parent object; they are specific subclasses implementing specialized functionality. Sometimes the common parent is the same class that contains the factory method.

Let's see an example implementation where we have:

- A common parent CarMaker constructor.
- A static method of the CarMaker called factory(), which creates car objects.
- Specialized constructors CarMaker.Compact, CarMaker.SUV, and CarMaker. Convertible that inherit from CarMaker. All of them will be defined as static properties of the parent so that we keep the global namespace clean, and so we also know where to find them when we need them.

Let's first see how the finished implementation will be used:

```
var corolla  = CarMaker.factory('Compact');
var solstice = CarMaker.factory('Convertible');
var cherokee = CarMaker.factory('SUV');
corolla.drive();  // "Vroom, I have 4 doors"
solstice.drive(); // "Vroom, I have 2 doors"
cherokee.drive(); // "Vroom, I have 17 doors"
```

This part:

```
var corolla = CarMaker.factory('Compact');
```

is probably the most recognizable in the factory pattern. You have a method that accepts a type given as a string at runtime and then creates and returns objects of the requested type. There are no constructors used with new or any object literals in sight, just a function that creates objects based on a type identified by a string.

Here's an example implementation of the factory pattern that would make the code in preceding snippet work:

```
// parent constructor
function CarMaker() {}

// a method of the parent
CarMaker.prototype.drive = function () {
    return "Vroom, I have " + this.doors + " doors";
};

// the static factory method
CarMaker.factory = function (type) {
    var constr = type,
        newcar;

    // error if the constructor doesn't exist
    if (typeof CarMaker[constr] !== "function") {
        throw {
            name: "Error",
            message: constr + " doesn't exist"
        };
    }

    // at this point the constructor is known to exist
    // let's have it inherit the parent but only once
    if (typeof CarMaker[constr].prototype.drive !== "function") {
```

```
        CarMaker[constr].prototype = new CarMaker();
    }
    // create a new instance
    newcar = new CarMaker[constr]();
    // optionally call some methods and then return...
    return newcar;
};

// define specific car makers
CarMaker.Compact = function () {
    this.doors = 4;
};
CarMaker.Convertible = function () {
    this.doors = 2;
};
CarMaker.SUV = function () {
    this.doors = 17;
};
```

There's nothing particularly difficult about the implementation of the factory pattern. All you need to do is look for the constructor function that creates an object of the required type. In this case a simple naming convention was used to map object types to the constructors that create them. The inheritance part was just an example of a common repeating piece of code that could be put into the factory method instead of repeated for every constructor type.

Built-in Object Factory

And for an example of "factory in the wild," consider the built-in global Object() constructor. It also behaves as a factory, because it creates different objects, depending on the input. If you pass it a primitive number, it can create an object with the Number() constructor behind the scenes. The same is true for the string and boolean values. Any other values, including no input values, will create a normal object.

Here are some examples and tests of the behavior. Note that Object can be called with or without new:

```
var o = new Object(),
    n = new Object(1),
    s = Object('1'),
    b = Object(true);

// test
o.constructor === Object;  // true
n.constructor === Number;  // true
s.constructor === String;  // true
b.constructor === Boolean; // true
```

The fact that Object() is also a factory is of little practical use, just something worth mentioning as an example that the factory pattern is all around us.

Iterator

In the iterator pattern, you have an object containing some sort of aggregate data. This data may be stored internally in a complex structure, and you want to provide easy access to each element of that structure. The consumer of your object doesn't need to know how you structure your data; all they need is to work with the individual elements.

In the iterator pattern, your object needs to provide a next() method. Calling next() in sequence must return the next consecutive element, where it's up to you to decide what "next" means in your particular data structure.

Assuming that your object is called agg, you could access each data element by simply calling next() in a loop like so:

```
var element;
while (element = agg.next()) {
    // do something with the element ...
    console.log(element);
}
```

In the iterator pattern, the aggregate object usually also provides a convenience has Next() method, so the users of the object can determine if they've reached the end of your data. Another way to access all elements sequentially, this time using hasNext(), would be the like the following:

```
while (agg.hasNext()) {
    // do something with the next element...
    console.log(agg.next());
}
```

Now that we have the use cases, let's see how to implement such an aggregate object.

When implementing the iterator pattern, it makes sense to privately store the data and a pointer (index) to the next available element. To demonstrate a sample implementation, let's assume the data is just an ordinary array and the "special" logic for retrieval the next consecutive element will be to return every other array element:

```
var agg = (function () {

    var index = 0,
        data = [1, 2, 3, 4, 5],
        length = data.length;

    return {

        next: function () {
            var element;
            if (!this.hasNext()) {
                return null;
            }
            element = data[index];
            index = index + 2;
            return element;
```

```
        },

        hasNext: function () {
            return index < length;
        }

    };
}());
```

To provide easier access and ability to iterate several times over the data, your object may provide additional convenience methods:

rewind()
> To reset the pointer back to the beginning

current()
> To return the current element, because you cannot do this with next() without advancing the pointer

Implementing those methods will not present any difficulty:

```
var agg = (function () {

    // [snip...]

    return {

        // [snip...]

        rewind: function () {
            index = 0;
        },
        current: function () {
            return data[index];
        }

    };
}());
```

Now testing the iterator:

```
// this loop logs 1, then 3, then 5
while (agg.hasNext()) {
    console.log(agg.next());
}

// go back
agg.rewind();
console.log(agg.current()); // 1
```

The result will be logging in the console: 1, 3, 5 (from the loop) and finally 1 (after the rewind).

Decorator

In the decorator pattern, additional functionality can be added to an object dynamically, at runtime. When dealing with static classes, this could be a challenge. In JavaScript, objects are mutable, so the process of adding functionality to an object is not a problem in itself.

A convenient feature of the decorator pattern is the customization and configuration of the expected behavior. You start with your plain object, which has some basic functionality. Then you pick and choose from an available pool of decorators which ones you want to use to enhance your plain object and in which order, if the order is important.

Usage

Let's take a look into an example usage of the pattern. Say you're working on a web application that sells something. Every new sale is a new `sale` object. The `sale` "knows" about the price of the item and can return it by calling the `sale.getPrice()` method. Depending on the circumstances, you can start decorating this object with extra functionality. Imagine a scenario where the sale for a customer is in the Canadian province of Québec. In this case the buyer needs to pay a federal tax and a provincial Québec tax. Following the decorator pattern, you'll say that you "decorate" the object with a federal tax decorator and a Québec tax decorator. You can then also decorate the object with price formatting functionality. This scenario could look like the following:

```
var sale = new Sale(100);         // the price is 100 dollars
sale = sale.decorate('fedtax');   // add federal tax
sale = sale.decorate('quebec');   // add provincial tax
sale = sale.decorate('money');    // format like money
sale.getPrice();                  // "$112.88"
```

In another scenario the buyer could be in a province that doesn't have a provincial tax, and you might also want to format the price using Canadian dollars, so you can do:

```
var sale = new Sale(100);         // the price is 100 dollars
sale = sale.decorate('fedtax');   // add federal tax
sale = sale.decorate('cdn');      // format using CDN
sale.getPrice();                  // "CDN$ 105.00"
```

As you can see, this is a flexible way to add functionality and tweak an object at runtime. Let's see how to approach an implementation of the pattern.

Implementation

One way to implement the decorator pattern is to have each decorator be an object containing the methods that should be overwritten. Each decorator actually inherits the object enhanced so far after the previous decorator. Each decorated method calls the same method on the uber (the inherited object) and gets the value and proceeds with doing something in addition.

The end effect is that when you do sale.getPrice() in the first usage example, you're calling the method of the money decorator (see Figure 7-1). But because each decorated method first calls the parent's method, money's getPrice() first calls quebec's getPrice(), which in turn calls fedtax's getPrice() and so on. The chain goes all the way up to the original undecorated getPrice() implemented by the Sale() constructor.

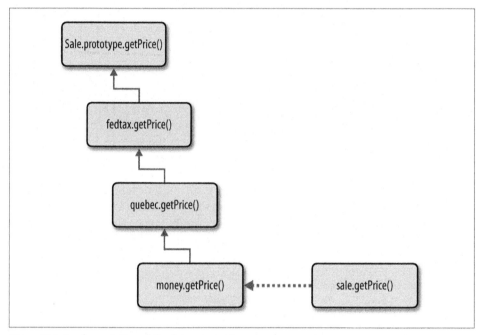

Figure 7-1. Implementation of the decorator pattern

The implementation starts with a constructor and a prototype method:

```
function Sale(price) {
    this.price = price || 100;
}
Sale.prototype.getPrice = function () {
    return this.price;
};
```

The decorator objects will all be implemented as properties of a constructor property:

```
Sale.decorators = {};
```

Let's see one example decorator. It's an object that implements the customized get Price() method. Note that the method first gets the value from the parent method and then modifies that value:

```
Sale.decorators.fedtax = {
    getPrice: function () {
        var price = this.uber.getPrice();
        price += price * 5 / 100;
        return price;
    }
};
```

Similarly we can implement other decorators, as many as needed. They can be extensions to the core Sale() functionality, implemented like plugins. They can even "live" in additional files and be developed and shared by third-party developers:

```
Sale.decorators.quebec = {
    getPrice: function () {
        var price = this.uber.getPrice();
        price += price * 7.5 / 100;
        return price;
    }
};

Sale.decorators.money = {
    getPrice: function () {
        return "$" + this.uber.getPrice().toFixed(2);
    }
};

Sale.decorators.cdn = {
    getPrice: function () {
        return "CDN$ " + this.uber.getPrice().toFixed(2);
    }
};
```

Finally let's see the "magic" method called decorate() that ties all the pieces together. Remember it will be called like:

```
sale = sale.decorate('fedtax');
```

The 'fedtax' string will correspond to an object that's implemented in Sale.decorators.fedtax. The newly decorated object newobj will inherit the object we have so far (either the original, or the one after the last decorator has been added), which is the object this. To do the inheritance part, let's use the temporary constructor pattern from the previous chapter. We also set the uber property of newobj so the children have access to the parent. Then we copy all the extra properties from the decorator to the newly decorated object newobj. At the end, newobj is returned and, in our concrete usage example, it becomes the new updated sale object:

```
Sale.prototype.decorate = function (decorator) {
    var F = function () {},
        overrides = this.constructor.decorators[decorator],
        i, newobj;
    F.prototype = this;
    newobj = new F();
    newobj.uber = F.prototype;
    for (i in overrides) {
```

```
            if (overrides.hasOwnProperty(i)) {
                newobj[i] = overrides[i];
            }
        }
        return newobj;
    };
```

Implementation Using a List

Let's explore a slightly different implementation, which benefits from the dynamic nature of JavaScript and doesn't need to use inheritance at all. Also instead of having each decorated method call the method previously in the chain, we can simply pass the result of the previous method as a parameter to the next method.

Such implementation could also allow for easy *undecorating* or undoing a decoration, which means simply removing an item from the list of decorators.

The usage example will be slightly simpler because we don't assign the return value from decorate() to the object. In this implementation, decorate() doesn't do anything to the object, it simply appends to a list:

```
var sale = new Sale(100); // the price is 100 dollars
sale.decorate('fedtax');  // add federal tax
sale.decorate('quebec');  // add provincial tax
sale.decorate('money');   // format like money
sale.getPrice();          // "$112.88"
```

The Sale() constructor now has a list of decorators as an own property:

```
function Sale(price) {
    this.price = price || 100;
    this.decorators_list = [];
}
```

The available decorators are once again implemented as properties of Sale.decorators. Note that the getPrice() methods are now simpler because they don't call the parent getPrice() to get the intermediate result; this result is passed to them as a parameter:

```
Sale.decorators = {};

Sale.decorators.fedtax = {
    getPrice: function (price) {
        return price + price * 5 / 100;
    }
};

Sale.decorators.quebec = {
    getPrice: function (price) {
        return price + price * 7.5 / 100;
    }
};

Sale.decorators.money = {
```

```
    getPrice: function (price) {
        return "$" + price.toFixed(2);
    }
};
```

The interesting part happens in the parent's `decorate()` and `getPrice()` methods. In the previous implementation, `decorate()` was somewhat complex and `getPrice()` was quite simple. In this implementation it's the other way around: `decorate()` just appends to a list while `getPrice()` does all the work. The work includes going through the list of currently added decorators and calling each of the `getPrice()` methods, passing the result from the previous:

```
Sale.prototype.decorate = function (decorator) {
    this.decorators_list.push(decorator);
};

Sale.prototype.getPrice = function () {
    var price = this.price,
        i,
        max = this.decorators_list.length,
        name;
    for (i = 0; i < max; i += 1) {
        name = this.decorators_list[i];
        price = Sale.decorators[name].getPrice(price);
    }
    return price;
};
```

This second implementation of the decorator pattern is simpler, and there's no inheritance involved. The decorating methods are also simpler. All the work is done by the method that "agrees" to be decorated. In this sample implementation, `getPrice()` is the only method that allows decoration. If you want to have more methods that can be decorated, then the part of going through the list of decorators should be repeated by each additional method. However, this can be easily abstracted into a helper method that takes a method and makes it "decoratable." In such an implementation the deco rators_list property would become an object with properties named after the methods and values being arrays of decorator objects.

Strategy

The strategy pattern enables you to select algorithms at runtime. The clients of your code can work with the same interface but pick from a number of available algorithms to handle their specific task depending on the *context* of what they are trying to do.

An example of using the strategy pattern would be solving the problem of form validation. You can create one validator object with a `validate()` method. This is the method that will be called regardless of the concrete type of form and will always return the same result—a list of data that didn't validate and any error messages.

But depending on the concrete form and the data to be validated, the clients of your validator may choose different types of checks. Your validator picks the best *strategy* to handle the task and delegates the concrete data checks to the appropriate algorithm.

Data Validation Example

Let's say you have the following piece of data, probably coming from a form on a page, and you want to verify whether it's valid:

```
var data = {
    first_name: "Super",
    last_name: "Man",
    age: "unknown",
    username: "o_0"
};
```

For the validator to know what is the best strategy to use in this concrete example, you need to configure the validator first and set the rules of what you consider to be valid and acceptable.

Let's say you will not require a last name and you'll accept anything for first name, but you require the age to be a number and the username to have letters and numbers only and no special symbols. The configuration will be something like:

```
validator.config = {
    first_name: 'isNonEmpty',
    age: 'isNumber',
    username: 'isAlphaNum'
};
```

Now that the `validator` object is configured to handle your data, you call its `validate()` method and print any validation errors to the console:

```
validator.validate(data);
if (validator.hasErrors()) {
    console.log(validator.messages.join("\n"));
}
```

This could print the following error messages:

```
Invalid value for *age*, the value can only be a valid number, e.g. 1, 3.14 or 2010
Invalid value for *username*, the value can only contain characters and numbers, no special
symbols
```

Now let's see how the validator is implemented. The available algorithms for the checks are objects with a predefined interface—they provide a `validate()` method and a one-line help information to be used in error messages:

```
// checks for non-empty values
validator.types.isNonEmpty = {
    validate: function (value) {
        return value !== "";
    },
    instructions: "the value cannot be empty"
```

```
};

// checks if a value is a number
validator.types.isNumber = {
    validate: function (value) {
        return !isNaN(value);
    },
    instructions: "the value can only be a valid number, e.g. 1, 3.14 or 2010"
};

// checks if the value contains only letters and numbers
validator.types.isAlphaNum = {
    validate: function (value) {
        return !/[^a-z0-9]/i.test(value);
    },
    instructions: "the value can only contain characters and numbers, no special symbols"
};
```

And finally the core of the validator object:

```
var validator = {

    // all available checks
    types: {},

    // error messages in the current
    // validation session
    messages: [],

    // current validation config
    // name: validation type
    config: {},

    // the interface method
    // `data` is key => value pairs
    validate: function (data) {

        var i, msg, type, checker, result_ok;

        // reset all messages
        this.messages = [];

        for (i in data) {

            if (data.hasOwnProperty(i)) {

                type = this.config[i];
                checker = this.types[type];

                if (!type) {
                    continue; // no need to validate
                }
                if (!checker) { // uh-oh
                    throw {
                        name: "ValidationError",
                        message: "No handler to validate type " + type
```

```
                };
            }

            result_ok = checker.validate(data[i]);
            if (!result_ok) {
                msg = "Invalid value for *" + i + "*, " + checker.instructions;
                this.messages.push(msg);
            }
        }
    }
    return this.hasErrors();
},

// helper
hasErrors: function () {
    return this.messages.length !== 0;
}
};
```

As you can see, the `validator` object is generic and could be kept like this for all validation use cases. The way to improve it would be to add more types of checks. If you use it on several pages, soon you'll have a nice collection of specific checks. Then all you need to do for each new use cases is to configure the validator and run the `validate()` method.

Façade

The façade is a simple pattern; it provides only an alternative interface to an object. It's a good design practice to keep your methods short and not have them handle too much work. Following this practice you'll end up with a greater number of methods than if you have *uber* methods with lots of parameters. Sometimes two or more methods may commonly be called together. In such cases it makes sense to create another method that wraps the repeating method calls.

For example, when handling browser events, you have the following methods:

`stopPropagation()`
> Traps the event and doesn't let it bubble up to the parent nodes

`preventDefault()`
> Doesn't let the browser do the default action (for example, following a link or submitting a form)

These are two separate methods with different purposes, and they should be kept separate, but at the same time, they are often called together. So instead of duplicating the two method calls all over the application, you can create a façade method that calls both of them:

```
var myevent = {
    // ...
    stop: function (e) {
```

```
            e.preventDefault();
            e.stopPropagation();
        }
        // ...
    };
```

The façade pattern is also suitable for browser scripting where the differences between
the browsers can be hidden behind a façade. Continuing from the previous example,
you can add the code that handles the differences in IE's event API:

```
    var myevent = {
        // ...
        stop: function (e) {
            // others
            if (typeof e.preventDefault === "function") {
                e.preventDefault();
            }
            if (typeof e.stopPropagation === "function") {
                e.stopPropagation();
            }
            // IE
            if (typeof e.returnValue === "boolean") {
                e.returnValue = false;
            }
            if (typeof e.cancelBubble === "boolean") {
                e.cancelBubble = true;
            }
        }
        // ...
    };
```

The façade pattern is also helpful with redesign and refactoring efforts. When you want
to replace an object with a different implementation, you have to do it over a period of
time (it's a complex object), while at the same time new code is being written that uses
this object. You can start with thinking about the new object's API and then proceed
to create a façade in front of the old object that follows the new API. This way, when
you get to fully replacing the old object, you'll have less client code to modify because
any recent client code will already use the new API.

Proxy

In the proxy design pattern, one object acts as an interface to another object. It's different from the façade pattern, where all you have is convenience methods that combine
several other method calls. The proxy sits between the client of an object and the object
itself and protects the access to that object.

This pattern may look like overhead but it's useful for performance purposes. The proxy
serves as a guardian of the object (also called a "real subject") and tries to have the real
subject do as little work as possible.

One example use would be something we can call *lazy initialization*. Imagine that initializing the real subject is expensive, and it happens that the client initializes it but never actually uses it. In this case the proxy can help by being the interface to the real subject. The proxy receives the initialization request but never passes it on until it's clear that the real subject is actually used.

Figure 7-2 illustrates the scenario where the client makes an initialization request and the proxy responds that all is good but doesn't actually pass on the message until it's obvious that the client needs some work done by the subject. Only then does the proxy pass both messages together.

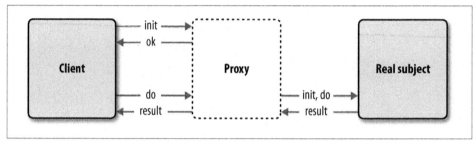

Figure 7-2. Relationship between client and real subject when going through a proxy

An Example

The proxy pattern is useful when the real subject does something expensive. In web applications, one of the most expensive operations you can do is a network request, so it makes sense to combine HTTP requests as much as possible. Let's take an example that does just that and demonstrates the proxy pattern in action.

A video expando

Let's have a little application that plays videos of a selected artist (Figure 7-3). You can actually play with the live example and look at the code at *http://www.jspatterns.com/book/7/proxy.html*.

You have a list of video titles on a page. When the user clicks a video title, the area below the title expands to show more information about the video and also enables the video to be played. The detailed video information and the URL of the video are not part of the page; they need to be retrieved by making a web service call. The web service can accept multiple video IDs, so we can speed up the application by making fewer HTTP requests whenever possible and retrieving data for several videos at one time.

Our application enables several (or all) videos to be expanded at the same time, so this is a perfect opportunity to combine web service requests.

Figure 7-3. Video expando in action

Without a proxy

The main "actors" in the application are the two objects:

videos
: Responsible for info areas expand/collapse (method `videos.getInfo()`) and playing videos (method `videos.getPlayer()`)

http
: Responsible for communication with the server via the method `http.makeRequest()`

When there's no proxy, `videos.getInfo()` will call `http.makeRequest()` once for every video. When we add a proxy, it will become a new actor called `proxy` and will be sitting between `videos` and `http` and delegating the calls to `makeRequest()`, combining them when possible.

Let's examine the code without the proxy first and then add the proxy to improve the responsiveness of the application.

HTML

The HTML code is just a list of links:

```
<p><span id="toggle-all">Toggle Checked</span></p>
<ol id="vids">
    <li><input type="checkbox" checked><a
        href="http://new.music.yahoo.com/videos/--2158073">Gravedigger</a></li>
    <li><input type="checkbox" checked><a
        href="http://new.music.yahoo.com/videos/--4472739">Save Me</a></li>
    <li><input type="checkbox" checked><a
        href="http://new.music.yahoo.com/videos/--45286339">Crush</a></li>
    <li><input type="checkbox" checked><a
        href="http://new.music.yahoo.com/videos/--2144530">Don't Drink The Water</a></li>
    <li><input type="checkbox" checked><a
        href="http://new.music.yahoo.com/videos/--217241800">Funny the Way It Is</a></li>
    <li><input type="checkbox" checked><a
        href="http://new.music.yahoo.com/videos/--2144532">What Would You Say</a></li>
</ol>
```

Event handlers

Now let's take a look at the event handlers. First we define the convenience shorthand $ function:

```
var $ = function (id) {
    return document.getElementById(id);
};
```

Using event delegation (more on this pattern in Chapter 8), let's handle all clicks occurring in the ordered list id="vids" with a single function:

```
$('vids').onclick = function (e) {
    var src, id;

    e = e || window.event;
    src = e.target || e.srcElement;

    if (src.nodeName !== "A") {
        return;
    }

    if (typeof e.preventDefault === "function") {
        e.preventDefault();
    }
    e.returnValue = false;

    id = src.href.split('--')[1];

    if (src.className === "play") {
        src.parentNode.innerHTML = videos.getPlayer(id);
        return;
```

```
        }
        src.parentNode.id = "v" + id;
        videos.getInfo(id);
    };
```

In the catch-all click handler we're interested in two clicks: one to expand/collapse the info section (calling getInfo()) and one to play the video (when the target has class name "play"), which means the info section has already been expanded, and we can then call getPlayer(). The IDs of the videos are extracted from the link hrefs.

The other click handler reacts to clicks to toggle all info sections. It's essentially just calling getInfo() again, but in a loop:

```
    $('toggle-all').onclick = function (e) {

        var hrefs,
            i,
            max,
            id;

        hrefs = $('vids').getElementsByTagName('a');
        for (i = 0, max = hrefs.length; i < max; i += 1) {
            // skip play links
            if (hrefs[i].className === "play") {
                continue;
            }
            // skip unchecked
            if (!hrefs[i].parentNode.firstChild.checked) {
                continue;
            }

            id = hrefs[i].href.split('--')[1];
            hrefs[i].parentNode.id = "v" + id;
            videos.getInfo(id);
        }
    };
```

videos object

The videos object has three methods:

getPlayer()
> Returns HTML required to play the Flash video (not relevant to the discussion).

updateList()
> The callback that receives all the data from the web service and produces HTML code to be used in the expanded info section. There's nothing particularly interesting happening in this method either.

getInfo()
> The method that toggles the visibility of the info sections and also makes the calls to http passing updateList() as a callback.

Here's a snippet of the object:

```
var videos = {

    getPlayer: function (id) {...},
    updateList: function (data) {...},

    getInfo: function (id) {

        var info = $('info' + id);

        if (!info) {
            http.makeRequest([id], "videos.updateList");
            return;
        }

        if (info.style.display === "none") {
            info.style.display = '';
        } else {
            info.style.display = 'none';
        }

    }
};
```

http object

The `http` object has only one method, which makes the JSONP request to Yahoo!'s YQL web service:

```
var http = {
    makeRequest: function (ids, callback) {
        var url = 'http://query.yahooapis.com/v1/public/yql?q=',
            sql = 'select * from music.video.id where ids IN ("%ID%")',
            format = "format=json",
            handler = "callback=" + callback,
            script = document.createElement('script');

        sql = sql.replace('%ID%', ids.join('","'));
        sql = encodeURIComponent(sql);

        url += sql + '&' + format + '&' + handler;
        script.src = url;

        document.body.appendChild(script);
    }
};
```

> YQL (Yahoo! Query Language) is a *meta* web service that offers the ability to use SQL-like syntax to consume a number of other web services without having to study each service's API.

When all six videos are toggled, six individual requests will be sent to the web service, with YQL queries that look like:

```
select * from music.video.id where ids IN ("2158073")
```

Enter the proxy

The code as previously described works just fine, but we can do better. The proxy object enters the scene and takes over the communication between http and videos. It tries to combine the requests using a simple logic: a 50ms buffer. The videos object does not call the HTTP service directly but calls the proxy instead. The proxy then waits before forwarding the request. If other calls from videos come in the 50ms waiting period, they will be merged into one. A delay of 50ms is pretty much imperceptible for the user but can help combine requests and speed up the experience when clicking "toggle" and expanding more than one video at once. It also reduces the server load significantly since the web server has to handle a smaller number of requests.

The combined YQL query for two videos will be like:

```
select * from music.video.id where ids IN ("2158073", "123456")
```

In the modified version of the code, the only change is that videos.getInfo() now calls proxy.makeRequest() instead of http.makeRequest(), as shown here:

```
proxy.makeRequest(id, videos.updateList, videos);
```

The proxy sets up a queue to collect the IDs of the videos received in the past 50ms and then flushes the queue calling http and provides its own callback function, because the videos.updateList() callback can handle only a single data record.

Here's the code for the proxy:

```
var proxy = {
    ids: [],
    delay: 50,
    timeout: null,
    callback: null,
    context: null,
    makeRequest: function (id, callback, context) {

        // add to the queue
        this.ids.push(id);

        this.callback = callback;
        this.context  = context;

        // set up timeout
        if (!this.timeout) {
            this.timeout = setTimeout(function () {
                proxy.flush();
            }, this.delay);
```

```
        }
    },
    flush: function () {

        http.makeRequest(this.ids, "proxy.handler");

        // clear timeout and queue
        this.timeout = null;
        this.ids = [];

    },
    handler: function (data) {
        var i, max;

        // single video
        if (parseInt(data.query.count, 10) === 1) {
            proxy.callback.call(proxy.context, data.query.results.Video);
            return;
        }

        // multiple videos
        for (i = 0, max = data.query.results.Video.length; i < max; i += 1) {
            proxy.callback.call(proxy.context, data.query.results.Video[i]);
        }
    }
};
```

Introducing the proxy provides the ability to combine multiple web service requests into one with only a simple change to the original code.

Figures 7-4 and 7-5 illustrate the scenarios of making three roundtrips to the server (without a proxy) versus one roundtrip when using a proxy.

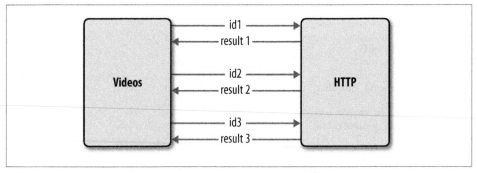

Figure 7-4. Three roundtrips to the server

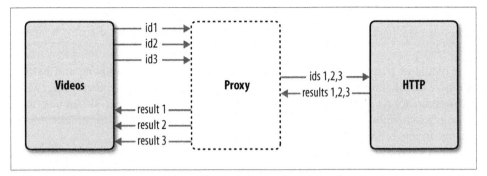

Figure 7-5. Using a proxy to combine and reduce the number of roundtrips to the server

Proxy As a Cache

In this example the client object (`videos`) was smart enough not to request the video information for the same video again. But that may not always be the case. The proxy can go further in protecting the real subject `http` by caching the results of previous requests into a new `cache` property (see Figure 7-6). Then if the `videos` object happens to request information about the same video ID for a second time, `proxy` can pull it out of the cache and save the network roundtrip.

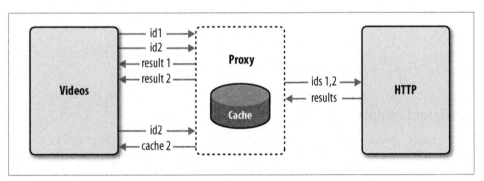

Figure 7-6. The proxy cache

Mediator

Applications—large and small—are made up of separate objects. All these objects need a way to communicate among themselves in a manner that doesn't hurt maintenance and your ability to safely change a part of the application without breaking the rest of it. As the application grows, you add more and more objects. Then, during refactoring, objects are removed and rearranged. When objects know too much about each other and communicate directly (call each other's methods and change properties) this leads to undesirable *tight coupling*. When objects are closely coupled, it's not easy to change one object without affecting many others. Then even the simplest change in an application is no longer trivial, and it's virtually impossible to estimate the time a change might take.

The mediator pattern alleviates this situation promoting *loose coupling* and helping improve maintainability (see Figure 7-7). In this pattern the independent objects (*colleagues*) do not communicate directly, but through a *mediator* object. When one of the colleagues changes state, it notifies the mediator, and the mediator communicates the change to any other colleagues that should know about it.

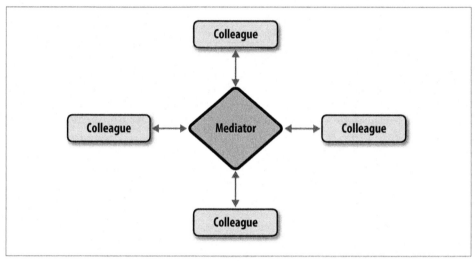

Figure 7-7. Participants in the mediator pattern

Mediator Example

Let's explore an example of using the mediator pattern. The application will be a game where two players are given half a minute to compete for who will press a button more times than the other. Player 1 competes by pressing 1 and player 2 presses 0 (so they are more comfortable and don't have to fight over the keyboard). A scoreboard is updated with the current score.

The participating objects will be:

- Player 1
- Player 2
- Scoreboard
- Mediator

The mediator knows about all other objects. It communicates with the input device (keyboard), handles keypress events, determines which player has a turn, and notifies it (see Figure 7-8). The player plays (meaning just updates its own score with one point) and notifies the mediator that he's done. The mediator communicates the updated score with the scoreboard, which in turn updates the display.

Other than the mediator, none of the other objects knows anything about any other object. That makes it trivial to update the game, for example, by adding a new player or another display showing the remaining time.

You can see the live version of the game and peek at the source at *http://jspatterns.com/book/7/mediator.html*.

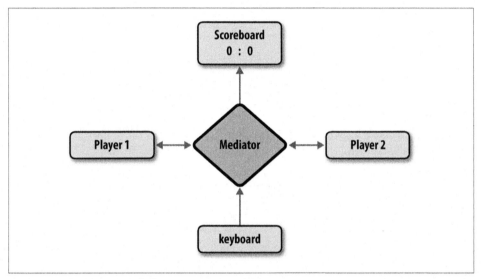

Figure 7-8. Participants in the keypress game

The player objects are created with a `Player()` constructor and have own properties `points` and `name`. The `play()` method from the prototype increments the points with one and then notifies the mediator:

```
function Player(name) {
    this.points = 0;
    this.name = name;
}
Player.prototype.play = function () {
    this.points += 1;
    mediator.played();
};
```

The `scoreboard` object has an `update()` method, which gets called by the mediator object after every player's turn. The scoreboard doesn't know about any players and doesn't keep score; it displays only the score given by the mediator:

```
var scoreboard = {

    // HTML element to be updated
    element: document.getElementById('results'),

    // update the score display
    update: function (score) {

        var i, msg = '';
        for (i in score) {
            if (score.hasOwnProperty(i)) {
                msg += '<p><strong>' + i + '<\/strong>: ';
                msg += score[i];
                msg += '<\/p>';
            }
        }
        this.element.innerHTML = msg;
    }
};
```

And now let's take a look at the `mediator` object. It initializes the game, creating player objects in its `setup()` method, and keeps track of the players in its `players` property. The `played()` method is called by each player after each turn. This method updates a `score` hash and sends it to the `scoreboard` for display. The last method, `keypress()`, handles the keyboard events, determines which player has a turn, and notifies it:

```
var mediator = {

    // all the players
    players: {},

    // initialization
    setup: function () {
        var players = this.players;
        players.home = new Player('Home');
        players.guest = new Player('Guest');

    },

    // someone plays, update the score
    played: function () {
        var players = this.players,
            score = {
                Home:  players.home.points,
                Guest: players.guest.points
            };

        scoreboard.update(score);
    },
```

```
        // handle user interactions
        keypress: function (e) {
            e = e || window.event; // IE
            if (e.which === 49) { // key "1"
                mediator.players.home.play();
                return;
            }
            if (e.which === 48) { // key "0"
                mediator.players.guest.play();
                return;
            }
        }
    };
```

And the last thing is to set up and tear down the game:

```
    // go!
    mediator.setup();
    window.onkeypress = mediator.keypress;

    // game over in 30 seconds
    setTimeout(function () {
        window.onkeypress = null;
        alert('Game over!');
    }, 30000);
```

Observer

The *observer* pattern is widely used in client-side JavaScript programming. All the browser events (mouseover, keypress, and so on) are examples of the pattern. Another name for it is also *custom events*, meaning events that you create programmatically, as opposed to the ones that the browser fires. Yet another name is *subscriber/publisher* pattern.

The main motivation behind this pattern is to promote loose coupling. Instead of one object calling another object's method, an object subscribes to another object's specific activity and gets notified. The subscriber is also called observer, while the object being observed is called publisher or subject. The publisher notifies (calls) all the subscribers when an important event occurs and may often pass a message in the form of an event object.

Example #1: Magazine Subscriptions

To understand how to implement this pattern, let's take a concrete example. Let's say you have a publisher paper, which publishes a daily newspaper and a monthly magazine. A subscriber joe will be notified whenever that happens.

The paper object needs to have a property subscribers that is an array storing all subscribers. The act of subscription is merely adding to this array. When an event occurs, paper loops through the list of subscribers and notifies them. The notification means calling a method of the subscriber object. Therefore, when subscribing, the subscriber provides one of its methods to paper's subscribe() method.

The paper can also provide unsubscribe(), which means removing from the array of subscribers. The last important method of paper is publish(), which will call the subscribers' methods. To summarize, a publisher object needs to have these members:

subscribers
    An array

subscribe()
    Add to the array of subscribers

unsubscribe()
    Remove from the subscribers array

publish()
    Loop though subscribers and call the methods they provided when they signed up

All the three methods need a type parameter, because a publisher may fire several events (publish both a magazine and a newspaper) and subscribers may chose to subscribe to one, but not to the other.

Because these members are generic for any publisher object, it makes sense to implement them as part of a separate object. Then we can copy them over (mix-in pattern) to any object and turn any given object into a publisher.

Here's an example implementation of the generic publisher functionality, which defines all the required members previously listed plus a helper visitSubscribers() method:

```
var publisher = {
    subscribers: {
        any: [] // event type: subscribers
    },
    subscribe: function (fn, type) {
        type = type || 'any';
        if (typeof this.subscribers[type] === "undefined") {
            this.subscribers[type] = [];
        }
        this.subscribers[type].push(fn);
    },
    unsubscribe: function (fn, type) {
        this.visitSubscribers('unsubscribe', fn, type);
    },
    publish: function (publication, type) {
        this.visitSubscribers('publish', publication, type);
    },
    visitSubscribers: function (action, arg, type) {
        var pubtype = type || 'any',
            subscribers = this.subscribers[pubtype],
            i,
            max = subscribers.length;

        for (i = 0; i < max; i += 1) {
```

```
            if (action === 'publish') {
                subscribers[i](arg);
            } else {
                if (subscribers[i] === arg) {
                    subscribers.splice(i, 1);
                }
            }
        }
    }
};
```

And here's a function that takes an object and turns it into a publisher by simply copying over the generic publisher's methods:

```
function makePublisher(o) {
    var i;
    for (i in publisher) {
        if (publisher.hasOwnProperty(i) && typeof publisher[i] === "function") {
            o[i] = publisher[i];
        }
    }
    o.subscribers = {any: []};
}
```

Now let's implement the paper object. All it can do is publish daily and monthly:

```
var paper = {
    daily: function () {
        this.publish("big news today");
    },
    monthly: function () {
        this.publish("interesting analysis", "monthly");
    }
};
```

Making paper a publisher:

```
makePublisher(paper);
```

Now that we have a publisher, let's see the subscriber object joe, which has two methods:

```
var joe = {
    drinkCoffee: function (paper) {
        console.log('Just read ' + paper);
    },
    sundayPreNap: function (monthly) {
        console.log('About to fall asleep reading this ' + monthly);
    }
};
```

Now the paper subscribes joe (in other words joe subscribes *to* the paper):

```
paper.subscribe(joe.drinkCoffee);
paper.subscribe(joe.sundayPreNap, 'monthly');
```

As you see, joe provides a method to be called for the default "any" event and another method to be called when the "monthly" type of event occurs. Now let's fire some events:

```
paper.daily();
paper.daily();
paper.daily();
paper.monthly();
```

All these publications call joe's appropriate methods and the result in the console is:

```
Just read big news today
Just read big news today
Just read big news today
About to fall asleep reading this interesting analysis
```

The good part here is that the paper object doesn't hardcode joe and joe doesn't hard-code paper. There's also no mediator object that knows everything. The participating objects are loosely coupled, and without modifying them at all, we can add many more subscribers to paper; also joe can unsubscribe at any time.

Let's take this example a step further and also make joe a publisher. (After all, with blogs and microblogs anyone can be a publisher.) So joe becomes a publisher and can post status updates on Twitter:

```
makePublisher(joe);
joe.tweet = function (msg) {
    this.publish(msg);
};
```

Now imagine that the paper's public relations department decides to read what its readers tweet and subscribes to joe, providing the method readTweets():

```
paper.readTweets = function (tweet) {
    alert('Call big meeting! Someone ' + tweet);
};
joe.subscribe(paper.readTweets);
```

Now as soon as joe tweets, the paper is alerted:

```
joe.tweet("hated the paper today");
```

The result is an alert: "Call big meeting! Someone hated the paper today."

You can see the full source code and play in the console with a live demo at *http://jspatterns.com/book/7/observer.html*.

Example #2: The Keypress Game

Let's take another example. We'll implement the same keypress game from the mediator pattern example but this time using the observer pattern. To make it slightly more advanced, let's accept an unlimited number of players, not only two. We'll still have the Player() constructor that creates player objects and the scoreboard object. Only the mediator will now become a game object.

In the mediator pattern the mediator object knows about all other participating objects and calls their methods. The game object in the observer pattern will not do that; instead it will leave it to the objects to subscribe to interesting events. For example, the scoreboard will subscribe to game's "scorechange" event.

Let's first revisit the generic publisher object and tweak its interface a bit to make it closer to the browser world:

- Instead of publish(), subscribe(), and unsubscribe(), we'll have fire(), on(), and remove().
- The type of event will be used all the time, so it becomes the first argument to the three functions.
- An extra context can be supplied in addition to the subscriber's function to allow the callback method to use this referring to its own object.

The new publisher object becomes:

```
var publisher = {
    subscribers: {
        any: []
    },
    on: function (type, fn, context) {
        type = type || 'any';
        fn = typeof fn === "function" ? fn : context[fn];

        if (typeof this.subscribers[type] === "undefined") {
            this.subscribers[type] = [];
        }
        this.subscribers[type].push({fn: fn, context: context || this});
    },
    remove: function (type, fn, context) {
        this.visitSubscribers('unsubscribe', type, fn, context);
    },
    fire: function (type, publication) {
        this.visitSubscribers('publish', type, publication);
    },
    visitSubscribers: function (action, type, arg, context) {
        var pubtype = type || 'any',
            subscribers = this.subscribers[pubtype],
            i,
            max = subscribers ? subscribers.length : 0;

        for (i = 0; i < max; i += 1) {
            if (action === 'publish') {
```

```
                subscribers[i].fn.call(subscribers[i].context, arg);
            } else {
                if (subscribers[i].fn === arg && subscribers[i].context === context) {
                    subscribers.splice(i, 1);
                }
            }
        }
    }
};
```

The new `Player()` constructor becomes:

```
function Player(name, key) {
    this.points = 0;
    this.name = name;
    this.key = key;
    this.fire('newplayer', this);
}

Player.prototype.play = function () {
    this.points += 1;
    this.fire('play', this);
};
```

The new parts here are that the constructor accepts `key`, the keyboard key that the player presses to make points. (The keys were hardcoded before.) Also, every time a new player object is created, an event "newplayer" is fired. Similarly, every time a player plays, the event "play" is fired.

The `scoreboard` object remains the same; it simply updates the display with the current score.

The new `game` object can keep track of all players, so it can produce a score and fire a "scorechange" event. It will also subscribe to all "keypress" events from the browser and will know about the keys that correspond to each player:

```
var game = {

    keys: {},

    addPlayer: function (player) {
        var key = player.key.toString().charCodeAt(0);
        this.keys[key] = player;
    },

    handleKeypress: function (e) {
        e = e || window.event; // IE
        if (game.keys[e.which]) {
            game.keys[e.which].play();
        }
    },

    handlePlay: function (player) {
        var i,
            players = this.keys,
```

```
            score = {};

    for (i in players) {
        if (players.hasOwnProperty(i)) {
            score[players[i].name] = players[i].points;
        }
    }
    this.fire('scorechange', score);
    }
};
```

The function makePublisher() that turns any object into a publisher is still the same as in the newspaper example. The game object becomes a publisher (so it can fire "score-change" events) and the Player.protoype becomes a publisher so that every player object can fire "play" and "newplayer" events to whomever decides to listen:

```
makePublisher(Player.prototype);
makePublisher(game);
```

The game object subscribes to "play" and "newplayer" events (and also "keypress" from the browser), while the scoreboard subscribes to "scorechange":

```
Player.prototype.on("newplayer", "addPlayer",  game);
Player.prototype.on("play",      "handlePlay", game);
game.on("scorechange", scoreboard.update, scoreboard);
window.onkeypress = game.handleKeypress;
```

As you see here, the on() method enables subscribers to specify the callback as a reference to a function (scoreboard.update) or as a string ("addPlayer"). The string works as long as the context (for example, game) is also provided.

The final bit of setup is to dynamically create player objects (with their corresponding keys to be pressed), as many as the user wants:

```
var playername, key;
while (1) {
    playername = prompt("Add player (name)");
    if (!playername) {
        break;
    }
    while (1) {
        key = prompt("Key for " + playername + "?");
        if (key) {
            break;
        }
    }
    new Player(playername,  key);
}
```

And that concludes the game. You can see the full source and play it at *http://jspatterns .com/book/7/observer-game.html*.

Notice that in the mediator pattern implementation, the mediator object had to know about every other object to call the correct methods at the right time and coordinate the whole game. Here the game object is a little dumber and relies on the objects observing certain events and taking action: for example, the `scoreboard` listening to the "scorechange" event. This results in an even looser coupling (the less one object knows, the better) at the price of making it a little harder to keep track of who listens to what event. In this example game, all the subscriptions happened in the same place in the code, but as an application grows, the `on()` calls may be all over the place (for example, in each object's initialization code). This will make it harder to debug, as there will be no single place to look at the code and understand what's going on. In the observer pattern, you move away from the procedural sequential code execution where you start from the beginning and can follow the program to the end.

Summary

In this chapter you learned about several popular design patterns and you saw how you could approach their implementation in JavaScript. The design patterns we discussed were:

Singleton
> Creating only one object of a "class." We looked at several approaches if you want to substitute the idea of a class with a constructor function and preserve the Java-like syntax. Otherwise, technically all objects in JavaScript are singletons. And also sometimes developers would say "singleton," meaning objects created with the module pattern.

Factory
> A method that creates objects of type specified as a string at runtime.

Iterator
> Providing an API to loop over and navigate around a complex custom data structure.

Decorator
> Tweaking objects at runtime by adding functionality from predefined decorator objects.

Strategy
> Keeping the same interface while selecting the best strategy to handle the specific task (context).

Façade
> Providing a more convenient API by wrapping common (or poorly designed) methods into a new one.

Proxy
> Wrapping an object to control the access to it, with the goal of avoiding expensive operations by either grouping them together or performing them only when really necessary.

Mediator

Promoting loose coupling by having your objects not "talk" to each other directly but only though a mediator object.

Observer

Loose coupling by creating "observable" objects that notify all their observers when an interesting event occurs (also called subscriber/publisher or "custom events").

CHAPTER 8

DOM and Browser Patterns

In the previous chapters of the book, the main focus was on the core JavaScript (ECMAScript) and not so much on patterns for using JavaScript in the browser. In contrast, this chapter explores a number of browser-specific patterns, because this is the most common environment for JavaScript programs. Browser scripting is also what most people have in mind when they say they don't like JavaScript. And that's understandable, given all the inconsistent host objects and DOM implementations that exist in the browsers. It's obvious that we can benefit from any good practices that help make the client scripting less of a pain.

In this chapter you see some patterns divided into several areas, including DOM scripting, event handling, remote scripting, strategies for loading JavaScript on the page, and steps to deploying JavaScript to production websites.

But first, let's start with a brief and somewhat philosophical discussion on how to approach client-side scripting.

Separation of Concerns

The three main concerns in web application development are:

Content
  The HTML document

Presentation
  The CSS styles that specify how the document looks

Behavior
  The JavaScript, which handles the user interaction and any dynamic changes to the document

Keeping the three concerns as separate as possible improves the delivery of the application to a vast array of user agents—graphic browsers, text-only browsers, assistive technology for disabled users, mobile devices, and so on. The *separation of concerns* also goes hand in hand with the idea of *progressive enhancement*—you start with the basic experience (HTML only) for the simplest user agents and add more to the experience as the user agent capabilities improve. If the browser supports CSS, then the user gets a better presentation of the document. If the browser supports JavaScript, then the document becomes more of an application that adds more features to enhance the experience.

In practice, the separation of concerns means:

- Testing the page with CSS turned off to see if the page is still usable and the content is present and readable
- Testing with JavaScript turned off and making sure the page can still perform its main purpose, all links work (no instances of `href="#"`), and any forms still work and submit properly
- Not using inline event handlers (such as `onclick`) or inline `style` attributes, because these do not belong to the content layer
- Using semantically meaningful HTML elements such as headings and lists

The JavaScript layer (the behavior) should be *unobtrusive,* meaning it shouldn't be in the way of the user, it shouldn't make the page unusable in unsupported browsers, and it shouldn't be a requirement for the page to work. Instead it should just enhance the page.

A common technique to handle browser differences elegantly is the *capability detection.* It suggests that you shouldn't use user agent sniffing to determine a code path, but you should check if a method or a property you want to use exists in the current environment. User agent sniffing is generally regarded as an antipattern. Sometimes it's unavoidable, but it should be the last resort and only in cases where capability detection cannot give a conclusive result (or will cause a significant performance hit):

```
// antipattern
if (navigator.userAgent.indexOf('MSIE') !== -1) {
    document.attachEvent('onclick', console.log);
}

// better
if (document.attachEvent) {
    document.attachEvent('onclick', console.log);
}

// or even more specific
if (typeof document.attachEvent !== "undefined") {
    document.attachEvent('onclick', console.log);
}
```

Separating concerns also helps development, maintenance, and ease of updates to an existing web application, because you know where to look when something breaks. When there's a JavaScript error, you don't need to look at the HTML or the CSS to fix it.

DOM Scripting

Working with the DOM tree of a page is one of the most common tasks in client-side JavaScript. This is also a major cause of headaches (and gives JavaScript a bad name) because the DOM methods are inconsistently implemented across browsers. That's why using a good JavaScript library, which abstracts the browser differences, can significantly speed up development.

Let's see some recommended patterns when accessing and modifying the DOM tree, mainly addressing performance concerns.

DOM Access

DOM access is expensive; it's the most common bottleneck when it comes to JavaScript performance. This is because the DOM is usually implemented separately from the JavaScript engine. From a browser's perspective, it makes sense to take this approach, because a JavaScript application may not need DOM at all. And also languages other than JavaScript (for example, VBScript in IE) can be used to work with the page's DOM.

The bottom line is that DOM access should be reduced to minimum. This means:

- Avoiding DOM access in loops
- Assigning DOM references to local variables and working with the locals
- Using selectors API where available
- Caching the `length` when iterating over HTML collections (see Chapter 2)

Consider the following example where the second (better) loop, despite being longer, will be tens to hundreds of times faster, depending on the browser:

```
// antipattern
for (var i = 0; i < 100; i += 1) {
    document.getElementById("result").innerHTML += i + ", ";
}

// better - update a local variable
var i, content = "";
for (i = 0; i < 100; i += 1) {
    content += i + ",";
}
document.getElementById("result").innerHTML += content;
```

In the next snippet, the second example (using a local variable `style`) is better, although it requires one more line of code and one more variable:

```
// antipattern
var padding = document.getElementById("result").style.padding,
    margin  = document.getElementById("result").style.margin;

// better
var style   = document.getElementById("result").style,
```

```
       padding = style.padding,
       margin  = style.margin;
```

Using selector APIs means using the methods:

```
document.querySelector("ul .selected");
document.querySelectorAll("#widget .class");
```

These methods accept a CSS selector string and return a list of DOM nodes that match
the selection. The selector methods are available in modern browsers (and in IE since
version 8) and will always be faster than if you do the selection yourself using other
DOM methods. Recent versions of popular JavaScript libraries take advantage of the
selector APIs, so you should make sure you use an up-to-date version of your preferred
library.

It will also help if you add id="" attributes to elements you'll be accessing often, because
document.getElementById(myid) is the easiest and fastest way to find a node.

DOM Manipulation

In addition to accessing the DOM elements, you often need to change them, remove
some of them, or add new ones. Updating the DOM can cause the browser to *repaint*
the screen and also often *reflow* (recalculate elements' geometry), which can be
expensive.

Again, the general rule of thumb is to have fewer DOM updates, which means batching
changes and performing them outside of the "live" document tree.

When you need to create a relatively big subtree, you should do so without adding to
the live document until the end. For this purpose you can use a *document fragment* to
contain all your nodes.

Here's how *not* to append nodes:

```
// antipattern
// appending nodes as they are created

var p, t;

p = document.createElement('p');
t = document.createTextNode('first paragraph');
p.appendChild(t);
document.body.appendChild(p);

p = document.createElement('p');
t = document.createTextNode('second paragraph');
p.appendChild(t);
document.body.appendChild(p);
```

A better version will be to create a document fragment, update it "offline," and add it
to the live DOM when it's ready. When you add a document fragment to the DOM
tree, the content of the fragment gets added, not the fragment itself. And this is really

convenient. So the document fragment is a good way to wrap a number of nodes even when you're not containing them in a suitable parent (for example, your paragraphs are not in a div element).

Here's an example of using a document fragment:

```
var p, t, frag;

frag = document.createDocumentFragment();

p = document.createElement('p');
t = document.createTextNode('first paragraph');
p.appendChild(t);
frag.appendChild(p);

p = document.createElement('p');
t = document.createTextNode('second paragraph');
p.appendChild(t);
frag.appendChild(p);

document.body.appendChild(frag);
```

In this example the live document is updated only once, causing a single reflow/repaint, as opposed to one for every paragraph, as was the case in the previous antipattern snippet.

The document fragment is useful when you *add* new nodes to the tree. But when you *update* an existing part of the tree, you can still batch changes. You can make a clone of the root of the subtree you're about to change, make all the changes to the clone, and then when you're done, swap the original with the clone:

```
var oldnode = document.getElementById('result'),
    clone = oldnode.cloneNode(true);

// work with the clone...

// when you're done:
oldnode.parentNode.replaceChild(clone, oldnode);
```

Events

Another area of browser scripting that is full of inconsistencies and a source of frustration is working with the browser events, such as click, mouseover, and so on. Again, a JavaScript library can take away much of the double work that needs to be done to support IE (before version 9) and the W3C-conforming implementations.

Let's go over the main points, because you may not always be using an existing library for simple pages and quick hacks, or you may be creating your own library.

Event Handling

It all starts with attaching event listeners to elements. Say you have a button that increments a counter each time you click it. You can add an inline `onclick` attribute and that will work across all browsers but will be violating the separation of concerns and the progressive enhancement. So you should strive for attaching the listener in JavaScript, outside of any markup.

Say you have the following markup:

```
<button id="clickme">Click me: 0</button>
```

You can assign a function to the `onclick` property of the node, but you can do this only once:

```
// suboptimal solution
var b = document.getElementById('clickme'),
    count = 0;
b.onclick = function () {
    count += 1;
    b.innerHTML = "Click me: " + count;
};
```

If you want to have several functions executed on click, you cannot do it with this pattern while maintaining loose coupling. Technically you can check if `onclick` already contains a function and if so, add the existing one to your own function and replace the `onclick` value with your new function. But a much cleaner solution is to use the `addEventListener()` method. This method doesn't exist in IE up to and including version 8, so you need `attachEvent()` for those browsers.

When we looked at the init-time branching pattern (Chapter 4) you saw an example of implementing a good solution for defining a cross-browser event listener utility. Without going into all the details right now, let's just attach a listener to our button:

```
var b = document.getElementById('clickme');
if (document.addEventListener) { // W3C
    b.addEventListener('click', myHandler, false);
} else if (document.attachEvent) { // IE
    b.attachEvent('onclick', myHandler);
} else { // last resort
    b.onclick = myHandler;
}
```

Now when this button is clicked, the function `myHandler()` will be executed. Let's have this function increment the number in the "Click me: 0" button label. To make it a little more interesting, let's assume we have several buttons and a single `myHandler()` for all of them. Keeping a reference to each button node and a counter for the number will be inefficient, given that we can get that information from the event object that is created on every click.

Let's see the solution first and comment on it after:

```
function myHandler(e) {

    var src, parts;

    // get event and source element
    e = e || window.event;
    src = e.target || e.srcElement;

    // actual work: update label
    parts = src.innerHTML.split(": ");
    parts[1] = parseInt(parts[1], 10) + 1;
    src.innerHTML = parts[0] + ": " + parts[1];

    // no bubble
    if (typeof e.stopPropagation === "function") {
        e.stopPropagation();
    }
    if (typeof e.cancelBubble !== "undefined") {
        e.cancelBubble = true;
    }

    // prevent default action
    if (typeof e.preventDefault === "function") {
        e.preventDefault();
    }
    if (typeof e.returnValue !== "undefined") {
        e.returnValue = false;
    }

}
```

A live example is available at *http://jspatterns.com/book/8/click.html*.

There are four parts in the event handler function:

- First, we need to gain access to the event object, which contains information about the event and the page element that triggered that event. This event object is passed to the callback event handler, but not when using the `onclick` property where it's accessible through the global property `window.event` instead.

- The second part is doing the actual work of updating the label.

- Next is canceling the propagation of the event. This is not required in this particular example, but in general if you don't do it, then the event bubbles up all the way to the document root or even the window object. Again we need to do it two ways: the W3C standard way (`stopPropagation()`) and then differently for IE (using `cancelBubble`).

- Finally, prevent the default action, if this is required. Some events (clicking a link, submitting a form) have default actions, but you can prevent them by using `preventDefault()` (or for IE, by setting `returnValue` to `false`).

As you see there's quite a bit of duplicate work involved, so it makes sense to create your event utility with façade methods as discussed in Chapter 7.

Event Delegation

The event delegation pattern benefits from the event bubbling and reduces the number of event listeners attached to separate nodes. If there are 10 buttons inside a `div` element, you can have one event listener attached to the `div` as opposed to 10 listeners attached to each button.

Let's have an example with three buttons inside a `div` (see Figure 8-1). A live demo of the event delegation example is available at *http://jspatterns.com/book/8/click-delegate .html*.

Figure 8-1. Event delegation example: three buttons that increment their labels on click

So we're working with the following markup:

```
<div id="click-wrap">
  <button>Click me: 0</button>
  <button>Click me too: 0</button>
  <button>Click me three: 0</button>
</div>
```

Instead of attaching listeners to each button, you attach one to the "click-wrap" `div`. Then you can use the same `myHandler()` function from the previous example with only one little change: you have to filter out clicks you're not interested in. In this case you look only for clicks on any button, so all other clicks in the same `div` could be ignored.

The change to `myHandler()` would be to check if the `nodeName` of the source of the event is a "button":

```
// ...
// get event and source element
e = e || window.event;
src = e.target || e.srcElement;

if (src.nodeName.toLowerCase() !== "button") {
    return;
}
// ...
```

The drawback of the event delegation is the slightly more code to filter out the events that happen in the container that are not interesting for you. But the benefits—performance and cleaner code—outweigh the drawbacks significantly, so it's a highly recommended pattern.

Modern JavaScript libraries make it easy to use event delegation by providing convenient APIs. For example YUI3 has the method `Y.delegate()`, which enables you to specify a CSS selector to match the wrapper and another selector to match the nodes you're interested in. This is convenient because your callback event handler function will actually never be called when the event happens outside the nodes you care about. In this case, the code to attach an event listener would be simply:

```
Y.delegate('click', myHandler, "#click-wrap", "button");
```

And thanks to the abstraction of all browser differences done in YUI and the fact that the source of the event is determined for us, the callback function will be much simpler:

```
function myHandler(e) {

    var src = e.currentTarget,
        parts;

    parts = src.get('innerHTML').split(": ");
    parts[1] = parseInt(parts[1], 10) + 1;
    src.set('innerHTML', parts[0] + ": " + parts[1]);

    e.halt();
}
```

A live example is available at: *http://jspatterns.com/book/8/click-y-delegate.html*.

Long-Running Scripts

You have noticed that sometimes the browser complains that a script has been running for too long and asks the user if the script should be stopped. You don't want this to happen in your application, no matter how complicated your task is.

Also, if the script works too hard, the browser's UI becomes unresponsive to the point where the user cannot click anything. This is bad for the experience and should be avoided.

In JavaScript there are no threads, but you can simulate them in the browser by using setTimeout() or, in more modern browsers, web workers.

setTimeout()

The idea is to split a big amount of work into smaller chunks and perform each chunk with a timeout of 1ms. Using 1ms timeout chunks can cause the task to be completed slower overall, but the user interface will remain responsive, and the user is more comfortable and in control of the browser.

Timeout of 1 (or even 0 milliseconds) will actually become more than that, depending on the browser and the operating system. Setting a 0 timeout doesn't mean right away, but rather "as soon as possible." In Internet Explorer, for example, the shortest clock "tick" is 15 milliseconds.

Web Workers

Recent browsers offer another solution to long-running scripts: web workers. Web workers provide background thread support in the browser. You put your heavy computations in a separate file, for example, *my_web_worker.js*, and then call it from the main program (page) like so:

```
var ww = new Worker('my_web_worker.js');
ww.onmessage = function (event) {
    document.body.innerHTML +=
        "<p>message from the background thread: " + event.data + "</p>";
};
```

The source for a web worker that does a simple arithmetic operation 1e8 times (1 with 8 zeros) is shown here:

```
var end = 1e8, tmp = 1;

postMessage('hello there');

while (end) {
    end -= 1;
    tmp += end;
    if (end === 5e7) { // 5e7 is the half of 1e8
        postMessage('halfway there, `tmp` is now ' + tmp);
    }
}

postMessage('all done');
```

The worker uses `postMessage()` to communicate with the caller and the caller subscribes to the `onmessage` event to receive updates. The `onmessage` callback receives an event object as an argument and this object contains the property `data`, which can be anything that the worker wants to pass. Similarly the caller can pass data to the worker using (in this example) `ww.postMessage()` and the worker can subscribe to those messages using an `onmessage` callback.

The previous example will print in the browser:

```
message from the background thread: hello there
message from the background thread: halfway there, `tmp` is now 3749999975000001
message from the background thread: all done
```

Remote Scripting

Today's web applications often use remote scripting to communicate with the server without reloading the current page. This enables for much more responsive and desktop-like web applications. Let's consider a few ways to communicate with the server from JavaScript.

XMLHttpRequest

XMLHttpRequest is a special object (a constructor function) available in most browsers today, which lets you make an HTTP request from JavaScript. There are three steps to making a request:

1. Set up an XMLHttpRequest object (called XHR for short).
2. Provide a callback function to be notified when the request object changes state.
3. Send the request.

The first step is as easy as:

```
var xhr = new XMLHttpRequest();
```

But in IE prior to version 7, the XHR functionality was implemented as an ActiveX object, so a special case is needed there.

The second step is providing a callback to the readystatechange event:

```
xhr.onreadystatechange = handleResponse;
```

The last step is to fire off the request—using two methods open() and send(). The open() method sets up the HTTP request method (for example, GET, POST) and the URL. The send() method passes any POST data or just a blank string in the case of GET. The last parameter to open() specifies whether the request is asynchronous. Asynchronous means that the browser will not block waiting for the response. This is definitely the better user experience, so unless there's a strong reason against it, the asynchronous parameter should always be true:

```
xhr.open("GET", "page.html", true);
xhr.send();
```

Below is a complete working example of fetching the contents of a new page and updating the current page with the new content (demo available at *http://jspatterns.com/book/8/xhr.html*):

```
var i, xhr, activeXids = [
    'MSXML2.XMLHTTP.3.0',
    'MSXML2.XMLHTTP',
    'Microsoft.XMLHTTP'
];

if (typeof XMLHttpRequest === "function") { // native XHR
    xhr = new XMLHttpRequest();
} else { // IE before 7
    for (i = 0; i < activeXids.length; i += 1) {
        try {
            xhr = new ActiveXObject(activeXids[i]);
            break;
        } catch (e) {}
    }
}
```

```
xhr.onreadystatechange = function () {
    if (xhr.readyState !== 4) {
        return false;
    }
    if (xhr.status !== 200) {
        alert("Error, status code: " + xhr.status);
        return false;
    }
    document.body.innerHTML += "<pre>" + xhr.responseText + "<\/pre>";
};

xhr.open("GET", "page.html", true);
xhr.send("");
```

Some comments on the example:

- Because of IE versions 6 and below, the process of creating a new XHR object is a little more complicated. We loop through a list of ActiveX identifiers from the latest to the earliest version and attempt to create an object, wrapping it in a try-catch block.

- The callback function checks the readyState property of the xhr object. There are five possible values of that property—from 0 to 4—where 4 means "complete." If the state is not yet complete, we keep waiting for the next readystatechange event.

- The callback also checks the status property of the xhr object. This property corresponds to the HTTP status code, for example, 200 (OK) or 404 (Not found). We're only interested in the 200 response codes and report all others as errors (for simplicity; otherwise there are other valid status codes you could check for).

- The code, as listed, will make a check for the supported way to create an XHR object every time a request is made. Having seen some patterns in previous chapters (for example, init-time branching), you could rewrite this to make the check only once.

JSONP

JSONP (JSON with padding) is another way to make remote requests. Unlike XHR, it's not restricted by the same-domain browser policy, so it should be used carefully because of the security implications of loading data from third-party sites.

The response to an XHR request can be any type of document:

- XML documents (historically)
- HTML chunks (quite common)
- JSON data (lightweight and convenient)
- Simple text files and others

With JSONP the data is most often JSON wrapped in a function call, where the function name is provided with the request.

An example JSONP request URL would commonly look like this:

http://example.org/getdata.php?callback=myHandler

getdata.php could be any type of page or script. The `callback` parameter specifies which JavaScript function will handle the response.

The URL is then loaded into a dynamic `<script>` element, like so:

```
var script = document.createElement("script");
script.src = url;
document.body.appendChild(script);
```

The server responds with some JSON data passed as a parameter to the callback function. The end result is that you've actually included a new script in the page, which happens to be a function call. For example:

```
myHandler({"hello": "world"});
```

JSONP example: Tic-tac-toe

Let's put the JSONP to work with an example—a game of tic-tac-toe, where the players are the client (the browser) and the server. Both will generate random numbers between 1 and 9, and we'll use JSONP to get the value of the server's turn (see Figure 8-2).

You can play the game live at *http://jspatterns.com/book/8/ttt.html*.

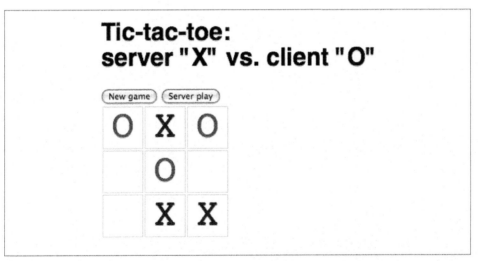

Figure 8-2. Tic-tac-toe JSONP challenge

There are two buttons: to start a new game and to get the server's turn (the client's turn will be automatic after a timeout):

```
<button id="new">New game</button>
<button id="server">Server play</button>
```

The board will contain nine table cells with corresponding `id` attributes. For example:

```
<td id="cell-1"> </td>
<td id="cell-2"> </td>
<td id="cell-3"> </td>
...
```

The whole game is implemented in a `ttt` global object:

```
var ttt = {
    // cells played so far
    played: [],

    // shorthand
    get: function (id) {
        return document.getElementById(id);
    },

    // handle clicks
    setup: function () {
        this.get('new').onclick = this.newGame;
        this.get('server').onclick = this.remoteRequest;
    },

    // clean the board
    newGame: function () {
        var tds = document.getElementsByTagName("td"),
            max = tds.length,
            i;
        for (i = 0; i < max; i += 1) {
            tds[i].innerHTML = " ";
        }
        ttt.played = [];
    },

    // make a request
    remoteRequest: function () {
        var script = document.createElement("script");
        script.src = "server.php?callback=ttt.serverPlay&played=" + ttt.played.join(',');
        document.body.appendChild(script);
    },

    // callback, server's turn to play
    serverPlay: function (data) {
        if (data.error) {
            alert(data.error);
            return;
        }
        data = parseInt(data, 10);
        this.played.push(data);

        this.get('cell-' + data).innerHTML = '<span class="server">X<\/span>';

        setTimeout(function () {
            ttt.clientPlay();
        }, 300); // as if thinking hard
```

```
    },

    // client's turn to play
    clientPlay: function () {
        var data = 5;

        if (this.played.length === 9) {
            alert("Game over");
            return;
        }

        // keep coming up with random numbers 1-9
        // until one not taken cell is found
        while (this.get('cell-' + data).innerHTML !== " ") {
            data = Math.ceil(Math.random() * 9);
        }
        this.get('cell-' + data).innerHTML = '0';
        this.played.push(data);

    }

};
```

The object `ttt` maintains a list of cells played so far in `ttt.played` and sends them to the server, so the server can return a new number excluding the ones that were already played. If an error occurs, the server will respond with output like:

```
ttt.serverPlay({"error": "Error description here"});
```

As you can see, the callback in JSONP has to be a publicly and globally available function, not necessarily a global, but it can be a method of a global object. If there are no errors, the server will respond with a method call like:

```
ttt.serverPlay(3);
```

Here 3 means that cell number 3 is the server's random choice. In this case the data is so simple that we don't even need the JSON format; a single value is all it takes.

Frames and Image Beacons

An alternative way to do remote scripting is to use frames. With JavaScript you can create an iframe and change its `src` URL. The new URL can contain data and function calls that update the caller—the parent page outside the iframe.

The simplest form of remote scripting is when all you need to do is to send data to the server, and you're not expecting a response. In those cases you can create a new image and point its `src` to the script on the server:

```
new Image().src = "http://example.org/some/page.php";
```

This pattern is called an *image beacon* and is useful when you want to send data to be logged by the server, for example for collecting visitor statistics. Because you have no use for a response of such a beacon, a common practice (but an antipattern) is to have the server respond with a 1×1 GIF image. A better option will be to respond with a "204 No Content" HTTP response. This means that only a header and no response body is sent back to the client.

Deploying JavaScript

There are a few performance considerations when it comes to serving JavaScript. Let's discuss the most important ones at a high level. For all the details, check *High Performance Web Sites* and *Even Faster Web Sites*, both published by O'Reilly.

Combining Scripts

The first rule when building fast-loading pages is to have as few external components as possible, because HTTP requests are expensive. When it comes to JavaScript, that means you can speed up the page loading times significantly by combining external script files together.

Let's say your page is using the jQuery library. This is one *.js* file. Then you're also using a few jQuery plugins, which also come each in a separate file. This way you can quickly end up with 4 or 5 files before you've written a single line. It makes sense to combine these files into one, especially given that some of them will be small in size (2 to 3 Kb) and the HTTP overhead will cost more time than the actual download. Combining the scripts simply means creating a new file and pasting the contents of each.

Of course, this concatenation of files should happen only right before the code goes to production and not in development, where it will make debugging more painful.

The drawbacks of combining script files are:

- It's one more step before going live, but it can easily be automated and done on the command line, for example using `cat` in Linux/Unix:

  ```
  $ cat jquery.js jquery.quickselect.js jquery.limit.js > all.js
  ```

- Losing some of the caching benefits—when you make a small change in one of the files, you invalidate the whole bundle. That's why it's good to have a release schedule for bigger projects or consider having two bundles: one that contains files that are expected to change and one "core" bundle that hardly changes at all.

- You need to come up with some naming and versioning pattern for the bundle, such as using a timestamp: *all_20100426.js* or a hash of the file's content.

The drawbacks can be summed up as mainly an inconvenience, but the benefit is well worth the trouble.

Minifying and Compressing

In Chapter 2 we talked about code minification. It's important to make the minification process also a part of your build go-live process.

When you think from the user perspective, there's no reason why they should have to download all the comments in your code, which serve no purpose for the way the application works.

The benefit of minification can be different depending on how generously you use comments and white space, and also on the specific minification tools you use. But on average you would be looking at around 50% file size reduction.

Serving the script file compressed is also something you should always do. It's a simple one-time server configuration to enable gzip compression, and it gives you an instant speed up. Even if you're using a shared hosting provider that doesn't give you much freedom in terms of server configuration, most providers at least allow you to use Apache's *.htaccess* configuration files. So in your web root, add this to the *.htaccess* file:

```
AddOutputFilterByType DEFLATE text/html text/css text/plain text/xml
application/javascript application/json
```

Compression will give you 70% smaller files on average. Combining compression with minification, you can expect your users to download a mere 15% of the file size of unminified, uncompressed source code you wrote.

Expires Header

Contrary to the popular belief, files do not get to stay for too long in the browser cache. You can do your due diligence and increase the chances of having your files in the cache for repeat visits by using an `Expires` header.

Again, this is a one-off server configuration you can do in *.htaccess*:

```
ExpiresActive On
ExpiresByType application/x-javascript "access plus 10 years"
```

The drawback is that if you want to change the file, you also need to rename it, but you'll probably be doing this already if you've established a naming convention for your bundles of combined files.

Using a CDN

CDN stands for Content Delivery Network. This is a paid (sometimes quite pricey) hosting service that lets you distribute copies of your files in different data centers around the world and have them served quicker to your users, while still keeping the same URL in your code.

Even if you don't have a budget for CDN, you can still benefit from some free options:

- Google hosts a number of popular open-source libraries, which you can link to for free and benefit from its CDN.
- Microsoft hosts jQuery and its own Ajax libraries.
- Yahoo! hosts YUI library on its CDN.

Loading Strategies

How you include a script in a web page seems like a straightforward question at a first glance—you use a `<script>` element and either inline the JavaScript code or link to a separate file in the `src` attribute:

```
// option 1
<script>
console.log("hello world");
</script>
// option 2
<script src="external.js"></script>
```

But there are some more patterns and considerations you should be aware of when your goal is building high-performance web applications.

As a side note, there are some common attributes developers tend to use with the `<script>` element:

language="JavaScript"
> In many forms of capitalizing "JavaScript" and sometimes with a version number. The `language` attribute shouldn't be used, because it's implied that the language is JavaScript. The version number doesn't work that well and is considered a mistake in retrospect.

type="text/javascript"
> This attribute is required by the HTML4 and XHTML1 standards, but it shouldn't be, because the browsers assume JavaScript anyway. HTML5 is making this attribute not required. Other than satisfying markup validators, there's no other reason to use the `type` attribute.

defer
> (And better yet, HTML5's `async`) is also a way, albeit not widely supported, to specify that downloading the external script file shouldn't block the rest of the page. More on blocking next.

The Place of the <script> Element

The script elements block progressive page downloads. Browsers download several components at a time, but when they encounter an external script, they stop further downloads until the script file is downloaded, parsed, and executed. This hurts the overall page time, especially if it happens several times during a page load.

To minimize the blocking effect, you can place the script element toward the end of the page, right before the closing `</body>` tag. This way there will be no other resources for the script to block. The rest of the page components will be downloaded and already engaging the user.

The worst antipattern is to use separate files in the head of the document:

```
<!doctype html>
<html>
<head>
    <title>My App</title>
    <!-- ANTIPATTERN -->
    <script src="jquery.js"></script>
    <script src="jquery.quickselect.js"></script>
    <script src="jquery.lightbox.js"></script>
    <script src="myapp.js"></script>
</head>
<body>
    ...
</body>
</html>
```

A better option is to combine all the files:

```
<!doctype html>
<html>
<head>
    <title>My App</title>
    <script src="all_20100426.js"></script>
</head>
<body>
    ...
</body>
</html>
```

And the best option is to put the combined script at the very end of the page:

```
<!doctype html>
<html>
<head>
    <title>My App</title>
</head>
<body>
    ...
    <script src="all_20100426.js"></script>
</body>
</html>
```

HTTP Chunking

The HTTP protocol supports the so-called chunked encoding. It enables you to send the page in pieces. So if you have a complicated page, you don't have to wait for all the server-side work to complete before you start sending the more or less static head of the page.

One simple strategy is to send the `<head>` content of the page with the first chunk while the rest of the page is being assembled. In other words you can have something like this:

```
<!doctype html>
<html>
<head>
    <title>My App</title>
</head>
<!-- end of chunk #1 -->
<body>
    ...
    <script src="all_20100426.js"></script>
</body>
</html>
<!-- end of chunk #2 -->
```

A simple improvement would be to also move the JavaScript back into the `<head>` and serve it with the first chunk. This way the browser has a head start downloading the script file while the rest of the page is not ready yet on the server side:

```
<!doctype html>
<html>
<head>
    <title>My App</title>
    <script src="all_20100426.js"></script>
</head>
<!-- end of chunk #1 -->
<body>
    ...
</body>
</html>
<!-- end of chunk #2 -->
```

An even better option would be to have a third chunk, which contains only the script at the very bottom of the page. You can also send a part of the body with the first chunk if you have a somewhat static header at the top of every page:

```
<!doctype html>
<html>
<head>
    <title>My App</title>
</head>
<body>
    <div id="header">
        <img src="logo.png" />
        ...
    </div>
    <!-- end of chunk #1 -->
```

```
    ... The full body of the page ...

    <!-- end of chunk #2 -->
    <script src="all_20100426.js"></script>
</body>
</html>
<!-- end of chunk #3 -->
```

This approach fits well in the spirit of progressive enhancement and unobtrusive Java-Script. Right after the end of the second chunk of HTML you should have a completely loaded, displayed, and usable page, just as if JavaScript were disabled in the browser. Then when the JavaScript arrives with the third chunk, it enhances the page, adding all the bells and whistles.

Dynamic <script> Element for Nonblocking Downloads

As mentioned already, JavaScript blocks the download of the files that follow it. But several patterns enable you to prevent this:

- Loading the script with an XHR request and then `eval()` it as a string. This approach suffers from same-domain restrictions and also involves `eval()`, which is an antipattern of itself.
- Using `defer` and `async` attributes, but these don't work across all browsers.
- Using a dynamic `<script>` element.

The last one is a good and doable pattern. Similar to what you saw with JSONP, you create a new script element, set its `src`, and append it to the page.

This is an example that will load a JavaScript file asynchronously without blocking the rest of the downloads:

```
var script = document.createElement("script");
script.src = "all_20100426.js";
document.documentElement.firstChild.appendChild(script);
```

The drawback of this pattern is that you cannot have any other script elements that follow this pattern if they rely on the main *.js* being loaded. The main *.js* is loaded asynchronously, so there's no guarantee when it will arrive, and the scripts that come after that might assume objects that are not yet defined.

To solve this drawback you can have all the inline scripts not execute right away but be collected as functions in an array. Then when the main script arrives, it can execute all the function collected in the buffer array. So there are three steps in achieving this.

First, create an array to store all inline code, as early in the page as possible:

```
var mynamespace = {
    inline_scripts: []
};
```

Then you need to wrap all the individual inline scripts into a function and append each function to the `inline_scripts` array. In other words:

```
// was:
// <script>console.log("I am inline");</script>

// becomes:
<script>
mynamespace.inline_scripts.push(function () {
    console.log("I am inline");
});
</script>
```

And the last step is to have your main script loop through the buffer of inline scripts and execute all of them:

```
var i, scripts = mynamespace.inline_scripts, max = scripts.length;
for (i = 0; i < max; max += 1) {
    scripts[i]();
}
```

Appending the <script> element

Commonly scripts are appended to the <head> of the document, but you can append them to any element, including the body (as with the JSONP example).

In the previous example we used `documentElement` to append to the <head>, because `documentElement` is the <html> and its first child is the <head>:

```
document.documentElement.firstChild.appendChild(script);
```

This is also commonly written as:

```
document.getElementsByTagName("head")[0].appendChild(script);
```

This is fine when you control the markup, but what if you're creating a widget or an ad and you have no idea what type of page will host it? Technically you may have no <head> and no <body> on the page; although `document.body` will most certainly work even without a <body> tag:

```
document.body.appendChild(script);
```

But there's actually one tag that will always exist on the page where your script is run—a script tag. If there were no script tag (for an inline or external file), then your code would not run. To use that fact you can `insertBefore()` the first available script element on the page:

```
var first_script = document.getElementsByTagName('script')[0];
first_script.parentNode.insertBefore(script, first_script);
```

Here `first_script` is the script element that's guaranteed to be on the page and `script` is the new script element you create.

Lazy-Loading

The technique known as lazy-loading refers to loading an external file after the page load event. It's often beneficial to split a large bundle of code into two parts:

- One part that is required for the page to initialize and attach event handlers to the UI elements
- A second part that is only needed after user interaction or other conditions

The goal is to load the page progressively and give the use something to work with as soon as possible. Then the rest can be loaded in the background while the user is engaged and looking around the page.

The way to load the second part of the JavaScript is again to simply use a dynamic script element appended to the head or the body:

```
... The full body of the page ...

<!-- end of chunk #2 -->
<script src="all_20100426.js"></script>
<script>
window.onload = function () {
    var script = document.createElement("script");
    script.src = "all_lazy_20100426.js";
    document.documentElement.firstChild.appendChild(script);
};
</script>
</body>
</html>
<!-- end of chunk #3 -->
```

For many applications, the lazy part of the code will most often be bigger than the core part, because the interesting "action" (such as drag and drop, XHR, and animations) happens only after the user initiates it.

Loading on Demand

The previous pattern loaded additional JavaScript unconditionally after page load, assuming that the code will likely be needed. But can we do better and load only parts of the code and only the parts that are really needed?

Imagine you have a sidebar on the page with different tabs. Clicking on a tab makes an XHR request to get content, updates the tab content, and animates the update fading the color. And what if this is the only place on the page you need your XHR and animation libraries, and what if the user never clicks on a tab?

Enter the load-on-demand pattern. You can create a `require()` function or method that takes a filename of a script to be loaded and a callback function to be executed when the additional script is loaded.

The require() function can be used like so:

```
require("extra.js", function () {
    functionDefinedInExtraJS();
});
```

Let's see how you can implement such a function. Requesting the additional script is straightforward—you just follow the dynamic `<script>` element pattern. Figuring out when the script is loaded is a little trickier due to the browser differences:

```
function require(file, callback) {

    var script = document.getElementsByTagName('script')[0],
        newjs = document.createElement('script');

    // IE
    newjs.onreadystatechange = function () {
        if (newjs.readyState === 'loaded' || newjs.readyState === 'complete') {
            newjs.onreadystatechange = null;
            callback();
        }
    };

    // others
    newjs.onload = function () {
        callback();
    };

    newjs.src = file;
    script.parentNode.insertBefore(newjs, script);
}
```

A few comments on this implementation:

- In IE you subscribe to the readystatechange event and look for a readyState "loaded" or "complete." All other browsers will ignore this.
- In Firefox, Safari, and Opera, you subscribe to the load event via the onload property.
- This approach doesn't work in Safari 2. If this browser is a requirement, to make it work there you'll have to set up an interval to periodically check if a specified variable (which you define in the additional file) has been defined. When it becomes defined, it means the new script has been loaded and executed.

You can test this implementation by creating an artificially delayed script (to simulate network latency), called *ondemand.js.php*, for example:

```
<?php
header('Content-Type: application/javascript');
sleep(1);
?>
function extraFunction(logthis) {
    console.log('loaded and executed');
    console.log(logthis);
}
```

Now testing the `require()` function:

```
require('ondemand.js.php', function () {
    extraFunction('loaded from the parent page');
    document.body.appendChild(document.createTextNode('done!'));
});
```

This snippet will write two lines to the console and update the page saying "done!" You can see the live example at *http://jspatterns.com/book/7/ondemand.html*.

Preloading JavaScript

In the lazy-loading pattern and the on-demand pattern, we post-load scripts required by the current page. In addition, you can also post-load scripts that are not needed on the current page but on the page that is likely to follow. This way, when the user lands on the second page, the user already has the script preloaded, and the overall experience becomes much faster.

Preloading can be implemented simply by using the dynamic script pattern. But this means that the script will be parsed and executed. Although parsing merely adds to the total time spent in preloading, the execution can additionally cause JavaScript errors when the preloaded script assumes it's running on the second page and, for example, expects to find certain DOM nodes.

It is possible to load scripts without parsing and executing them; this works for CSS and images, too.

In IE you can make a request with the familiar image beacon pattern:

```
new Image().src = "preloadme.js";
```

In all other browsers you can use an `<object>` instead of a script element and set its data attribute to point to the URL of the script:

```
var obj = document.createElement('object');
obj.data = "preloadme.js";
document.body.appendChild(obj);
```

To prevent the object from being visible, you should also set its `width` and `height` attributes to 0.

You can create a general-purpose `preload()` function or method and also use the init-time branching pattern (Chapter 4) to handle the browser differences:

```
var preload;
if (/*@cc_on!@*/false) { // IE sniffing with conditional comments
    preload = function (file) {
        new Image().src = file;
    };
} else {
    preload = function (file) {
        var obj = document.createElement('object'),
            body = document.body;
```

```
        obj.width = 0;
        obj.height = 0;
        obj.data = file;
        body.appendChild(obj);
    };
}
```

Using the new function:

```
preload('my_web_worker.js');
```

The drawback of this pattern is the presence of user agent sniffing, but it cannot be avoided because, in this case, the capability detection doesn't tell us enough about the browser behavior. In this pattern, for example, theoretically you can test if typeof Image is a "function" and use that instead of the sniffing. However this won't help here, because all browsers support new Image(); it's just that some have a separate cache for images, which means that preloading components as an image will not be used as a script from the cache on the second page but will be downloaded again.

 Browser sniffing using conditional comments is interesting in itself. It is slightly safer than looking for strings in navigator.userAgent, because these strings are easy to change by the user.

Having this:

```
var isIE = /*@cc_on!@*/false;
```

will set isIE to false in all browsers (because they ignore the comment), but it will be true in Internet Explorer, because of the negation ! in the conditional comment. It's as if IE sees:

```
var isIE = !false; // true
```

The preloading pattern can be used for all kinds of components, not only scripts. It's useful, for example, on login pages. When the user starts typing his or her username, you can use this typing time to start preloading (nothing sensitive, of course), because it's likely that the user will end up on the second logged-in page.

Summary

Whereas the previous chapters in the book covered mostly JavaScript core patterns, independent of the environment, this one focused on patterns applicable only in the client-side browser environment.

We looked at:

- The ideas of separation of concerns (HTML: content, CSS: presentation, Java-Script: behavior), unobtrusive JavaScript, and capability detection versus browser sniffing. (Although toward the end of the chapter you learned how to break this pattern.)

- DOM scripting—patterns to speed up DOM access and manipulation, mainly by batching DOM operations together because touching the DOM always comes at a cost.

- Events, cross-browser event handling, and using event delegation to reduce the number of event listeners and improve performance.

- Two patterns for handling cases of long-running heavy computations—using `set Timeout()` to break long operations into smaller chunks and using web workers in modern browsers.

- Various patterns for remote scripting and communication between server and client—XHR, JSONP, frames and image beacons.

- Steps to deploy JavaScript in production environment—making sure the scripts are combined into fewer files, minified and gzipped (85% total savings), and ideally hosted on a CDN and sent with `Expires` header to improve caching.

- Patterns for including the scripts on a page for best performance, including: various places to put the `<script>` element, while also benefiting from HTTP chunking. Also in order to reduce the initial "hit" of loading a big script we looked at various patterns such as lazy-loading, preloading, and on-demand loading JavaScript.

Index

We'd like to hear your suggestions for improving our indexes. Send email to *index@oreilly.com*.

variables, 101
  (see also global variables)
  declaring, 11
  defined, 10
  defining, 3
  hoisting, 14, 61
  local, 58
  naming conventions, 28
  scope considerations, 58
  typecasting, 21–23

W

web workers, 190
white space (coding convention), 26, 27, 36
wildcards, sandbox pattern and, 102, 105
window property, 10, 13
wrapper objects, 52

X

XMLHttpRequest object, 191, 192

Y

YAHOO global variable (YUI2), 90
Yahoo! YUICompressor, 36
YQL web service, 164
YUI (Yahoo! User Interface) library, 31, 127
YUIDoc tool, 30, 31–34

Z

Zakas, Nicholas, 16

About the Author

Stoyan Stefanov is a Yahoo! web developer, book author (*Object-Oriented Java-Script*), book contributor (*Even Faster Web Sites, High Performance JavaScript*), and technical reviewer (*JavaScript: The Good Parts, PHP Mashups*). He speaks regularly about JavaScript, PHP, and other web development topics at conferences and on his blog (*http://www.phpied.com*). Stoyan is the creator of the smush.it image optimization tool and architect of Yahoo's performance optimization tool YSlow 2.0.

Colophon

The animal on the cover of *JavaScript Patterns* is a European partridge (*Perdix perdix*), also called a gray partridge, English partridge, Hungarian partridge, or Bohemian partridge. This widespread bird is native to Europe and western Asia, but it has been introduced in North America and is now common in some parts of southern Canada and the northern United States.

Partridges are members of the pheasant family, Phasianidae. They are nonmigratory ground-nesters that eat mainly grain and seeds. Originally residents of grasslands, they became adapted to and spread with human agriculture; they are now most often found near cultivated fields.

European partridges are rotund, chicken-like birds (about 12 inches long) with short necks and tails. They have brown backs, gray underparts (with a dark chestnut belly patch), rusty faces, and dull bills and legs. Their clutches, consisting of 15 to 20 eggs, are among the largest of any bird. Widely introduced as gamebirds, partridges were extensively hunted in the late 1800s and early 1900s.

The bird's scientific name comes from Perdix of Greek mythology, the nephew of the inventor Daedalus. Daedalus was jealous of his young student—credited with having invented the saw, the chisel, the geometric compass, and the potter's wheel—and seized an opportunity to shove him off of the Acropolis. Athena, sympathetic to the clever boy, came to his rescue and turned him into a partridge, a bird that avoids heights and prefers to nest on the ground.

The cover image is from *Johnson's Natural History*. The cover font is Adobe ITC Garamond. The text font is Linotype Birka; the heading font is Adobe Myriad Condensed; and the code font is LucasFont's TheSansMonoCondensed.

Get even more for your money.

Join the O'Reilly Community, and register the O'Reilly books you own. It's free, and you'll get:

- $4.99 ebook upgrade offer
- 40% upgrade offer on O'Reilly print books
- Membership discounts on books and events
- Free lifetime updates to ebooks and videos
- Multiple ebook formats, DRM FREE
- Participation in the O'Reilly community
- Newsletters
- Account management
- 100% Satisfaction Guarantee

Signing up is easy:

1. **Go to: oreilly.com/go/register**
2. **Create an O'Reilly login.**
3. **Provide your address.**
4. **Register your books.**

Note: English-language books only

To order books online:
oreilly.com/store

For questions about products or an order:
orders@oreilly.com

To sign up to get topic-specific email announcements and/or news about upcoming books, conferences, special offers, and new technologies:
elists@oreilly.com

For technical questions about book content:
booktech@oreilly.com

To submit new book proposals to our editors:
proposals@oreilly.com

O'Reilly books are available in multiple DRM-free ebook formats. For more information:
oreilly.com/ebooks

O'REILLY®

Spreading the knowledge of innovators   oreilly.com

The information you need, when and where you need it.

With Safari Books Online, you can:

Access the contents of thousands of technology and business books

- Quickly search over 7000 books and certification guides
- Download whole books or chapters in PDF format, at no extra cost, to print or read on the go
- Copy and paste code
- Save up to 35% on O'Reilly print books
- **New!** Access mobile-friendly books directly from cell phones and mobile devices

Stay up-to-date on emerging topics before the books are published

- Get on-demand access to evolving manuscripts.
- Interact directly with authors of upcoming books

Explore thousands of hours of video on technology and design topics

- Learn from expert video tutorials
- Watch and replay recorded conference sessions